From my perspective and vantage point, as I travel all over the land from coast to coast, I see many people doing certain things their way and expecting a benefit or blessing. As we approach the critical crossroads on our journey through uncertain times in these latter days, it may become easy to get caught up in the confusion and chaos of the moment. But if we can acquire a vision we will see clearly the path and choose the right road when we arrive at the critical crossroads. For there really is only one way!

THERE IS
ONLY ONE WAY
AMEN!

ISBN 0-9767079-4-2

ISBN 0-9767079-4-2

Dedication

A very special dedication to all people who have chosen to Obey and keep the Commandments of our One True Most High God. You have remained committed and into the word each and every day seeking and getting truth and practicing truth. As we journey on into these latter days we know who can lead us through the perilous times ahead, if we will only come in through the door and follow the one true path to prosperity and eternal life. We know that your life has been and must continue to be a special and shining example to all those who have watched you or come in contact with you over your precious life. You know the way and have continued to help others find the way just as you have from our One True Most High God.

You are a true believer, and you have studied to shew thyself approved unto God, a workman that needeth not to be ashamed, rightly dividing the word of truth, as stated in II Timothy 2:15.

You know that as stated in Job 36:11 that if they obey and serve him, they shall spend their days in prosperity, and their years in pleasures. This book is specially dedicated to you, the true believers and doers of the word. You have stood up and taken action when it may not have been popular to do so. You know that in order for a people to be exalted that they must proceed in a righteous direction. You have chosen your companions wisely and will benefit from the type of companions you choose, and not to become unequally yoked together with unbelievers. You have borne your burden well into the heat of the day.

You know that we are in the fig tree generation and that there will be perilous times as we journey deeper and deeper into these latter days. But you know the way and will stand up and let your light so shine and be the example you were chosen to be.

You have stood up and took action and gotten to the conclusion of the whole matter, and know your duty as stated in Ecclesiastes 12:13. For the true believers know that there is Only One Way as stated in St. John 14:6.

Thomas J. Pyatt

Contents

iii

There is Only One Way, AMEN!

Introduction

Many people have stated and believe that there is more than one way to accomplish anything in life, and they see various ways to accomplish their goals and objectives. That may be true for many things that are carnal or secular; but we all have a spiritual side and must know and recognize this. Yet, many people keep fighting their spiritual leanings in favor of walking in the flesh and after the flesh. But our warfare is not carnal, and we are now in these latter days in the midst of a spiritual war. I am convinced that it is Only The One True Most High God that can get us safely through these perilous days to come. There is Only One Way for us to get there as so eloquently stated in St. John 14:6. But too many people are still trying to do it their way and are stuck on the bottom of the mud pile wallowing in disillusionment.

We have all seen people keep doing things their way and everyone just says, well that's just her or him, and that's how they've always done it. But the critical question should be asked, is it scriptural and God's way? Many people have been doing things their way so long because of the traditions of men (Colossians 2:8) and following the commandments of men (St. Mark 7:7). But we are told what we should be doing in St. Matthew 7:7 and we only have to ask, seek and knock. We must put on the new man and leave the old man behind, and get a renewed spirit of the mind (Ephesians 4:23-24).

People are destroyed for lack of knowledge (Hosea 4:6, Proverbs 13:20) therefore, you must choose your companions wisely. Be partakers of the light and not darkness, and don't become unequally yoked (II Corinthians (6:14-18). We should not judge any man but we should all be able to discern the righteous from the wicked, from him that serveth God from him that serveth him not, as stated in Malachi 3:18. I believe that the workers of iniquity will be destroyed (Psalm 5:5, 7:11, 145:20).

I believe that the Scriptures-Holy Bible is true, and that holy men spoke as they were moved by God and that all scripture is given by inspiration of God (II Peter 1:21, II Timothy 3:16). Who? But the One True Most High God could have foretold us over 2,000 years ago exactly what would happen here in this last generation-fig tree generation in these latter days. We know we are in the fig tree generation and we know what half and what quarter we are in! We were told what would happen to the land and countries we reside in today. We know what land is the king of the south and why he will continue to push on as foretold in the Book of Daniel. We know we have been foretold exactly what will happen here in our fig tree generation.

How could man have foretold our future so accurately so many millenniums ago? We have been foretold all things as stated in St. Mark 13:23. I know that I must put on the Whole Armour of God and Be a Doer of The Word in order to make it safely through these perilous times here in these latter days. Let us Hearken!

Hearken, before it's too late. There is someone calling for your Attention, Commitment and Time. And you will listen, stand up and proceed in a righteous and holy manner. You will ACT and put on the new man with a new mindset. You have heard the call, just answer the call! Your Attention, Commitment and Time is needed.

Attention – Your Attention is needed
Commitment – Your Commitment is needed
Time – Your Time is needed

Listen, let us get to the Conclusion of the whole matter and Do our duty; for There really is Only One Way (Ecclesiastes 12:13, St. John 14:6).

I am a servant of the One True Most High God.

There is Only One True Most High God

There is Only One Way, and that way has been given to us by the One True Most High God. As we get deeper and deeper into these latter days we see troubles all around as perilous times keep a-coming. Many people are searching for answers and seeking a way to go, serving their own gods or going their own way, but troubles keep a-coming. We all should be servants to the Most High God for there is Only One True God. There is Only One True God and one mediator between God and men; and that mediator is Jesus Christ (I Timothy 2:5). There is none other and none else besides the One True God (Isaiah 45:5-7). Jesus said "I am the way, the truth, and the life: no man cometh unto the Father, but by me" (St. John 14:6). He is our comforter and can fill all our needs in these times of great stress as we labour and are heavy laden (St. Matthew 11:28-30). We have been foretold all things; so let us do our whole duty (St. Mark 13:23, Ecclesiastes 12:13).

There is Only One Way as stated in St. John 14:6. Let us all be Doers of the Word and fulfill the condition precedent in Deuteronomy 28:13. We must put on the whole armour of God to be protected as we journey deeper into these latter days (Ephesians 6:11-13). Many will feel the fervent heat as the elements melt all around them. They must know that there is Only One True God that can save them from the snares and wiles of the rulers of the darkness of the world (Jeremiah 10:10-15, Psalm 90:2, Revelation 1:7-8).

Can a Man Walk Through the Fire and Not Get Burned

Many people are walking and roaming all over the land in these troubled and perilous times, and many are still trying to walk it alone. Walking through these difficult times alone is like trying to walk through the fire alone. We all need protection as we roam and walk deeper and deeper into these latter days, and there is only one way we can get the protection we need. The critical question was asked in Proverbs 6:27, "Can a man take fire in his bosom, and his clothes not be burned?"

For ages people have been trying to go through the fire of difficult situations alone, and were destroyed. Many people are not prepared for the battles of these latter days, and people are destroyed for a lack of knowledge (Hosea 4:6). As we get deeper into these latter days many people will feel the fervent heat as the elements melt all around them. They must know that a man cannot walk through the fire and not get burned without having the protection of the One True God. He will walk with you and protect you if you will only call on him and keep his Commandments, Statutes and Laws, as we were told to do. He was with Shadrach, Meshach, and Abednego when they were tossed into the burning fiery furnace for refusing to worship a false god, that golden image that Nebuchadnezzar the king had set up.

Only three were tossed into the burning fiery furnace, but there in the midst of the furnace were four, and the form of the fourth is like the Son of God. The door to the fiery furnace was opened and Shadrach, Meshach, and Abednego came out unharmed; for the fire had no power over their bodies because they had the protection

5

of the One True God (Daniel 3:1-30). There is Only One Way to have complete protection as we walk through these difficult situations that will destroy you if you walk alone (Deuteronomy 28:15-45, II Peter 2:9, 3:10, Isaiah 24:6, St. John 14:6).

You can get the Knowledge you need and should get it because people are destroyed for lack of Knowledge.

People are Destroyed for a Lack of Knowledge

We were told to get Wisdom, Knowledge and Understanding, and that it came from a higher source (Proverbs 1:7, 2:6, 3:5, 4:7). With Knowledge we can acquire the skills and expertise to solve many pressing problems facing our communities today. Many people have got their own way of doing things and will not even consider applying scriptural solutions to solve the problems facing them today. There are many troubling problems in our depressed communities today, such as, a high crime rate, a high dropout rate, and insufficient economic skills to compete in the global economy. Large portions of our cities are being laid waste with empty storehouses. People are being Destroyed for a Lack of Knowledge (Hosea 4:6).

Many ask the question, can a change come? Well, just look in the mirror and start there, and be Doers of the Word (James 1:22-25). There is Only One Way to The

Truth and The Life, and we must remain connected to the One True Vine (St. John 14:6, 15:1). W can become clean through the word which was spoken to us (St. John 15:3). We are the branches and must remain connected to the One True Vine in order to bear good fruit. If we fall to the ground the branches will become withered, and men will use the withered branches to start a fire. We know that no man can walk through the fire and not get burned without the protection of the One True God. We know that the keeping of all of God's Commandments, Statutes and Laws is Wisdom, Knowledge and Understanding (Job 28:28, Psalm 111:10).

We must hearken to the Commandments of the Lord our God, to Observe and to Do them (Deuteronomy 28:13). Let us not wander and be destroyed for a lack of knowledge (Proverbs 13:20, Psalm 5:5, 7:11, 145:20). For there is Only One Way, so let us put on the whole armour of God and be Doers of the word (Ephesians 6:11-13, St. John 14:6).

There is Only One Way, as we were told millenniums ago.

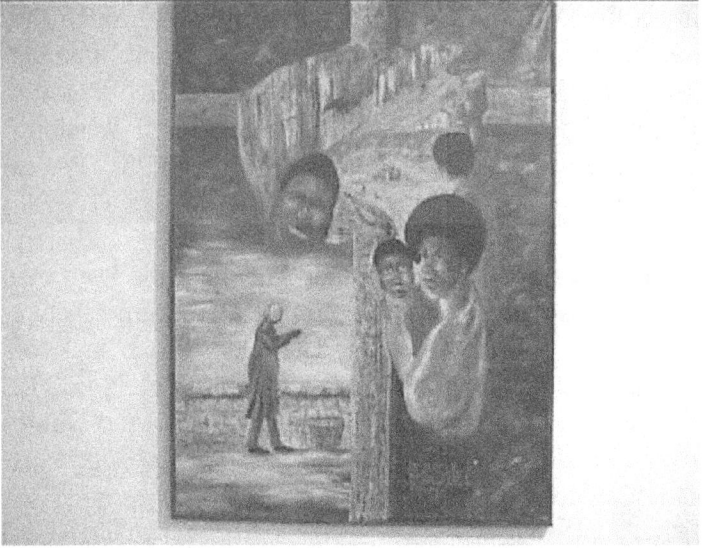

There is Only One Way

There is Only One (1) Way

As I watched many different athletic events on television with people holding many signs and on many occasions a sign which read, John 3:16. There is a very powerful message in that verse and one to live by and never forget. But, we must **understand** that this verse is not the only thing that we must do, if we would just back up to John 3:3 which says that, Except a man be **born again**, he cannot see the kingdom of God. I Peter 1:23 tell us that "**Being born again**, not of corruptible seed, but of incorruptible, **by the word of God**, which liveth and abideth for ever." Therefore, we must read and study (and rightly divide) the word of God to know what we should do to have life and have life more abundantly as so eloquently stated in St. John 10:10. And also that every man should eat and drink, and enjoy the good of all his labour, it is the gift of God, Ecclesiastes 3:13.

And **St. John 14:6** tells us the way, and this is the **Only Way.**

We must also **Keep, Abide By, and Do The Commandments** – Deuteronomy 28:1-14, Ecclesiastes 12:13-14, St. Matthew 19:17, St. Matthew 22:36-40, St. John 14:15, Revelation 22:7, Revelation 22:14.

Exodus Chapter 20 and Deuteronomy Chapter 5 give us the **10 Commandments**. Deuteronomy 28:1-14 tells us all the blessings that we will receive if we observe and do all the commandments and statutes. We will be the head and not the tail, we will be above and not beneath. There are also curses for disobedience as stated in

9

Deuteronomy 28:15-68. We are told in Leviticus 11:44-45 and I Peter 1:15-16 to be holy. It is a surety that we will all be rewarded according to our works, Revelation 20:12 and 22:12. There is **Only One Way** and **St. John 14:6** tells us the way. Remember what Jesus said in St. John 14:15, "If ye love me, keep my commandments".

As we sojourn through the latter years in the fig tree generation we know that many false prophets shall arise and deceive many, for we have been foretold all things, and the signs of the end tell us this, St. Matthew 24:, St. Mark 13:, and St. Luke 21. We are also warned of false prophets in Ezekiel 13: and 34: and Jeremiah 23: and 14:14-15, and II Peter 2:. Many will be deceived because they are seeking the easy way out and want to do it their way or want to rely on someone else to do it for them or tell them what to do. Deuteronomy 18:15-22 tells you how to recognize your true prophet and where he will come from. But, there is **only one mediator between God and men**, I Timothy 2:5.

Proverbs 1:7, 4:7, 2:6, and 3:5, tell us to get wisdom, knowledge and understanding, and tell us who is the only one who can give us such wisdom, knowledge and understanding. **There is Only One Way** as stated in **St. John 14:6.**

I will Put on the Whole Armour of God and Be a Doer of The Word.

Put On The Whole Armour Of God

The sun is setting deeper and deeper into these latter days as the devil is roaming with his many wiles to deceive those unprepared and unprotected or proceeding under false pretenses. The devil knows that he has but a short time to tarry here and knows who he can attack, he knows his wiles can deceive those that forget God and turns their face from God; he knows that any nation that forgets God shall perish (Deuteronomy 8:19-20, Daniel 9:11-14). Sometimes people or a nation forgets who gave them what they have and brought them to a land that lacks nothing, and gave them their land to live in peace and freedom (Deuteronomy 8:1-18).

We have many wonderful schools all over our land, and people the world over keep coming here to seek a better life for themselves and their children. Many of us have degrees and skills and believe that we are smart; but we have kicked God out of our schools, and then send our children to those same schools expecting those schools to teach our children wisdom and knowledge to solve the major problems of the world and our community. Our schools are going down and deteriorating with violence and mass shootings, the drop out rate is increasing and the literacy rate is decreasing. Many people are wondering what is the problem and are implementing what they think will solve the problems. We even go to athletic events and sing God bless us. But we kicked God out of our schools; and the devil knows that his wiles will succeed where God is not present. The one true God will restore his people if they return to him.

If we turn our face from God then God will hide his face

from us, and trouble will abound all over with terrors within, the Song of Moses tells us this (Deuteronomy 32:). As we get deeper into the latter days more troubles keep coming with various terrors. Is there a terror war or is it a spiritual war, a war against principalities, powers, the rulers of the darkness of this world with spiritual wickedness in high places? (Ephesians 6:11-12). Who is their god? When a war has false religious underpinnings and is deeply embedded in such false teachings throughout with spiritual wickedness in high places, it is really a spiritual war. Man cannot defeat the devil alone, for we wrestle not against flesh and blood, therefore our bombs cannot kill or destroy the devil's wiles. We must put on the whole armour of God (Ephesians 6:11-13).

A spiritual war is full of terror with the devil's wiles. We must "take the shield of faith, to be able to quench all the fiery darts of the wicked" (Ephesians 6:16). There is a spiritual war here deep in these latter days, the righteous versus the wicked. Who is their god, there is only one true God and one true vine, and there is none other beside the true God (II Timothy 2:5, Isaiah 45: 5-7, St. John 15:1). There is only one way (St. John 14:6). Let us put on and "take the helmet of salvation, and the sword of the Spirit, which is the word of God" (Ephesians 6:17). This is a spiritual war, full of the devil's wiles, he beguiled Eve in the Garden of Eden, and he'll beguile you too if you don't have on the whole armour of God.

To survive a spiritual war and the devil's wiles, we must "Put on the whole armour of God, that ye may be able to stand against the wiles of the devil" (Ephesians) 6:11-13). We cannot kick God out and prevail (Deuteronomy 8:20, Daniel 9:11-14). For there really is only one way, so let us do our duty (St. John 14:6, Ecclesiastes 12:13).

Be a Doer of The Word

1. **Keep (DO and Observe) All The Commandments, Statutes and Laws.** (Exodus 20:1-17, Deuteronomy 5:7-22, 6:1-2, 8:1-11, 18-20, 9:10-11, 11:26-28, 28:1,13, James 1:22-25, Ephesians 2:8, I Peter 1:23-25, St. John 14:6, 15, Ecclesiastes 12:13).

2. **Study and Work.** (II Timothy 2:15, I Thessalonians 4:11, II Thessalonians 3:6-12, St. Matthew 5:16, 16:27, Psalm 62:12, James 2:17-26, Revelation 20:12, 22:12, Proverbs 13:11, 20:4, Ecclesiastes 3:13, Galatians 6:7).

3. **Get Wisdom, Knowledge and Understanding.** (Proverbs 1:7, 4:7, 2:6, 3:5, Job 28:28, Psalm 111:10, II Peter 1:21, II Timothy 3:16).

4. **Don't Follow Vain Persons.** (Proverbs 28:19, 12:11, Ephesians 5:6, Romans 6:23, Psalm 5:5, 7:11, 145:20, II Peter 2:9, Proverbs 26:11, II Corinthians 11:13-15, Malachi 3:18, James 4:7).

5. **Get a Renewed spirit of the mind.** (Ephesians 4:23-24, Colossians 3:10).

6. **Abide in The True Vine.** (St. John 15:1-11, 3:3-5, 3:16, 10:10, 14:6).

7. **Practice Truth, Teach Truth, Know The Truth.** (St. Matthew 7:7, 11:28-30, 28:19-20, St. Mark 7:7, St. John 8:32, 10:9, 14:6).

Commandments, Laws and Statutes

Commandments

Exodus 20: & Deuteronomy 5: - The Ten Commandments

Laws

Exodus 12:	-	Law of the Passover
Exodus 21:	-	Laws about Murder
Exodus 22:	-	Laws about Property
Exodus 23:	-	Laws of the Sabbath
Leviticus 2: & 7:	-	The Law of Meat Offerings
Leviticus 3: & 7:	-	The Law of Peace Offerings
Leviticus 4:, 5:,7:	-	The Sin Offering
Leviticus 6: & 7:	-	The Burnt Offering
Leviticus 7:	-	The Trespass Offering
Leviticus 11:	-	The Law of Clean and Unclean
Deuteronomy 14:	-	" " " " "
Leviticus 12: & 13:	-	Laws about Skin Plagues
Leviticus 15:	-	Laws about Uncleanness
Leviticus 18:	-	Laws about Unlawful Sexual Relations
Deuteronomy 22:	-	" " "
Leviticus 19:	-	Laws of Personal Conduct
Leviticus 20:	-	Punishments for Sin
Leviticus 26:	-	Blessings for Obedience – Results of Disobedience
Deuteronomy 14: & 22:	-	Laws about Tithes
Deuteronomy 21:	-	Miscellaneous Laws
Deuteronomy 22:	-	Laws of Sexual Conduct

Deuteronomy 24:	-	Various Laws (Moses divorcement law)
Deuteronomy 28:	-	Blessings of Obedience – Curses of Disobedience
Deuteronomy 11:26-28	-	" " "
Deuteronomy 32:	-	Song of Moses
Psalm 37:	-	Righteous Blessed
Ecclesiastes 12:13	-	The Whole Duty of Man

Be a Doer of The Word, for All are Not Saved.

ALL ARE NOT SAVED (Rev. 21:8)

There will be a new Heaven and a new Earth (Rev.21:1). The elements of the old earth shall melt (II Peter 3:12).

We have been foretold all things (Mark 13:23). God reveals to his servants (Amos 3:7).

FAITH – (James 2:17-20)   Salvation . . .   Milk v. Meat (Hebrews 5:13, 14)

Solutions to our problems are detailed in God's word – Holy Scriptures.

POVERTY – (Proverbs 28:19, 12:11, 13:18, 20:4 sluggard).
Abraham and Jacob were very rich and wealthy (Genesis 13:2, 30:43).

WORK – (Proverbs 28:19, 12:11, 26:14, 20:4) (I Thes. 4:11, II Thes. 3:10-12) (Eccle. 3:13) Reward according to your works (Rev. 22:12, 20:12).

WICKED SHALL BE DESTROYED – (Psalm 37:20, 73:19, 145:20) (Rev. 21:8) (Proverbs 24:16) (Isaiah 48:22, 57:21).   The Song of Moses.
Watchman's Duty to warn the wicked (Ezekiel 33:)

FOOLS PERISH – Not inherit the Earth. (Proverbs 1:, 10:, 14:24, 22:9, 26:11, 26:4, 27:12).

Man must be Born Again (I Peter 1:23, John 3:3-5, Galatians 6:7)

LETTERS TO SEVEN CHURCHES - Teach Truth!

16

LETTERS TO SEVEN CHURCHES -
(not Denominations) Teach Truth

1. Ephesus   -   Thou hast left thy first love.
Remember therefore from whence thou
art fallen, and **repent**, and do the first
works;

2. Smyrna   -   I know thy works and tribulation, and
poverty (but thou art rich) . . .

3. Pergamos -   Thou hast them that hold the doctrine
of Balaam, . . . and doctrine of
Nicolaitanes. **Repent**; or else I will
come unto thee quickly, . . .

4. Thyatira   -   Thou sufferest Jezebel, which callest
herself a prophetess, to teach and
seduce my servants to commit
fornication, and she repented not.
Them that commit adultery with her,
repent of their deeds. I will give unto
every one of you according to your
works.

5. Sardis   -   I have not found thy works perfect
before God. **Repent**. I will come on
thee as a thief, . . . I know thy works:
behold: A few are worthy...

6. Philadelphia – I have set before thee an <u>open door</u>, and no man can shut it. Because thou has kept the word of my patience, I will also keep thee from the hour of temptation, which shall come upon all the world, to try them that dwell upon the earth.

7. Laodicea - I know thy works, that thou art neither cold nor hot: thou art **lukewarm,** . . . Thou sayest I am rich, . . . and have need of nothing. Behold, I stand at the door, and knock: if any man hear my voice, and open the door. I will come in to him . . .

You Say You Have Been Saved?
But Have You Heard The Conclusion
Of The Whole Matter?

Saved   -   We are told how to be saved in St. John 3:16-17, Acts 16:30-31, Ephesians 2:5. But that is not all we were told we must do!

Born Again - St. John 3:3 tells us that, "Except a man be born again, he cannot see the kingdom of God". I Peter 1:23 tell us how to be born again by the word of God.

Be Holy   -   Leviticus 11:44-45 and I Peter 1:15-16 tells us to be holy!

Do   -   In Deuteronomy 28:1-14
Commandments   Ecclesiastes 12:13-14, St. John 14:15, Revelation 22:14 we are told to Observe and Do All the Commandments and Statutes of God. This is a condition to receiving your blessings and reward. All nations are blessed in Abraham; and Abraham, Isaac and Jacob were very wealthy and prosperous.

There's   -   St. John 14:6 tells us the Only Way,
Only 1 Way   I Timothy 2:5 tell us there's Only One Mediator between God and men. In St. John 14:15 Jesus tells you what you would do if you loved him.

Reward - Revelation 20:12, 22:12, tell us that we will all be rewarded according to our works!

Righteous - We are told that the righteous will be
Blessed blessed and the wicked cut off! Psalm 37:, Deuteronomy 28:1-14, Deuteronomy 28:15-68, Ezekiel 33:, Malachi 3:18. Repent and Forsake!

Poverty - We need not end up or remain in poverty. Proverbs 28:19, 12:11, 13:18, 13:11, 11:31, Deuteronomy 28:13. The destruction of the poor is their poverty, Proverbs 10:15. Hearken to your true prophet, Deuteronomy 18:15-22.

Conclusion - Listen, Do you understand Your Duty? Have you done Your Duty? Ecclesiastes 12:13-14.

8 Days In The Beginning

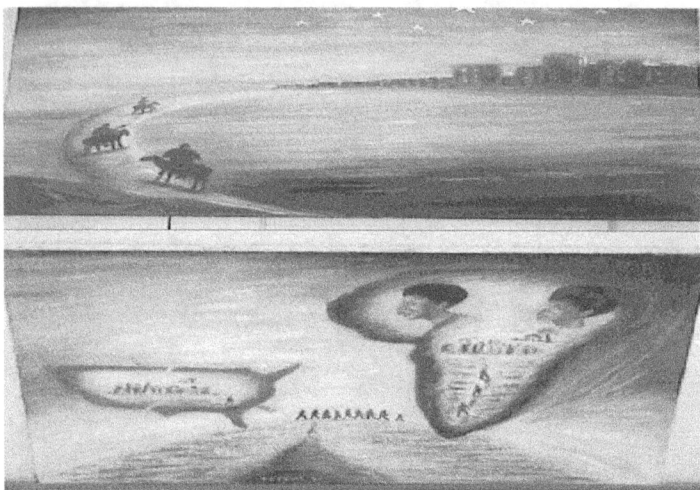

Let Us Seek Wisdom, Knowledge and
Understanding; Just as in the Days of Old

GET WISDOM, KNOWLEDGE and UNDERSTANDING

We can be prosperous and healthy, and not hooked on drugs, alcohol or other mind twisters. We need not be in or remain in poverty. Analyze the Word!
Analyze the Word!

The first chapter of Proverbs tells us that fools despise instruction and knowledge, and that fools have no wisdom or understanding. Proverbs 4:7 tell us to get Wisdom and Understanding. Proverbs 2:6 tell us that the Lord giveth Wisdom and Understanding. Proverbs 3:5 tell us to trust in the Lord with all thine heart, and lean not unto thine own understanding.

The Word is the Truth, and if we practice the Truth we will be rewarded accordingly, for each and every one shall be rewarded according to their works. The Word contains specific modus operandi's to solve problems and avoid problems and undesired situations. Proverbs 28:19, 12:11, 13:18, tells us how to avoid poverty. Leviticus Chapter 11 gives us the law of the beasts, clean and unclean animals, and tells us that eating unclean animals will defile the body.

The Word is Truth, so practice Truth and know the Truth. There are consequences for disobedience, for ALL ARE NOT SAVED (Psalms 37:, 73: Rev. 21:8). Analyze the Word! The solutions to our problems have already been given to us in the Word. The way has already been prepared. We need not be afraid when perilous times come, for we know that the day of the Lord is a day of darkness, no light (Joel & Amos). We have been given the signs of the end (Matthew 24: Mark

23

13: Luke 21:) so we should not be deceived by false teachers, but many shall be deceived.

I Timothy 2:5 tell us that there is only one mediator between God and men. So beware of false shepherds as described in (Ezekiel 34: Jeremiah 10:21, 23:1-4). In Deuteronomy 18:15-22 God said he would raise us up a Prophet from among our brethren (18:15 says, The Lord thy God will raise up unto thee a Prophet from the midst of thee, of thy brethren, like unto me; unto him ye shall hearken;). Analyze the Word!
Analyze the Word!

We have an obligation to help the poor and those with infirmities. But we have no obligation to help fools or lazy people (Proverbs 26:11, 26:14, II Thessalonians 3:10). Many people are seeking benefits (freeloaders), but do not want to assume their responsibilities and obligations. Many have been strategically misadjusted, and have degrees but no economic skills. Therefore it becomes difficult to obtain ownership and control of the economic entities in our communities. We continue to beg and seek government aid and expect others to do for us what we should do for ourselves. No one will develop your community for you, but you!

We refuse to turn over $ dollars in our communities or support businesses owned by members of our communities. Such foolishness will only ensure that we will be systematically manipulated into economic dependency on others outside the community, and continue to remain on the bottom of the economic ladder.

We have so called educated people, who are good speakers, and they have meetings, form committees, and

24

talk forever, but no pragmatic action is being taken to establish an Economic Agenda for the community. Degrees alone are not sufficient, economic skills and a pooling of resources is also needed. The owner of a laundry has more economic sense than many people with degrees who have no economic agenda for their communities. Such a wanton and reckless disregard for logic and common sense only insures that one will suffer the natural and probable consequences of their actions. Does your shepherd have an economic agenda based on the Word? Analyze the Word!

The Word is Truth, and we should Practice Truth. Listen to what the Spirit is saying to the seven churches (Revelation 1:-3:). These seven philosophies are here today (no matter what name or denomination they call themselves). Their works will identify them. Only 2 of the 7 churches were acceptable to God (Smyrna & Philadelphia). Is your philosophy the same as these 2? Four of the other five churches were told to Repent, and the 5th was lukewarm, neither cold nor hot, so it got spit out.

As we approach the day of darkness, the critical crossroads will appear, and we must decide what direction we will take for ALL ARE NOT SAVED (Rev. 21:8). Malachi 3:18 tells us to discern between the righteous and the wicked, between him that serveth God and him that serveth him not. Ezekiel 13:22 tell us not to strengthen the hand of the wicked by promising him life. We should make the right decision, for we have been foretold all things (Mark 13:23). The Word is Truth, and we should Practice Truth.   Analyze the Word!

YOU CAN BE PROSPEROUS AND HEALTHY
(Not Strategically Misadjusted to Be Happy in Poverty and on the Bottom)

In the midst of the community is a mindset not based on the WORD or TRUTH. It is a mindset based on the world, without priorities and out of sync and full of false teachings, fads and foolish logic. It's all too common to hear comments like, my baby's daddy is coming, or my baby's mamma said, or to see too many people wandering or hanging around hooked on mindtwisters.

Many have been strategically misadjusted or miseducated to the point of accepting:
1. The Abnormal for the Normal
2. Fiction for Facts, and
3. Folly for wisdom . . .

Many are still being taught to accept their condition in life and that this is the way things were intended to be. But the WORD says otherwise! God gives us a specific modus operandi with detailed specifics on how to be Healthy and Prosperous and avoid Poverty. We have been given Health Laws that tells us what animals are clean and unclean in Leviticus Chapter 11, and that eating unclean animals will defile the body. Proverbs 28:19, 12:11 and 13:18 tells us how to avoid poverty. Ecclesiastes 3:13 states, And also that every man should eat and drink, and enjoy the good of all his labour, it is the gift of God. Proverbs 11:31 states, Behold, the righteous shall be recompensed in the earth: much more the wicked and the sinner. This means that you can be rewarded in the flesh while you are here on earth.

But you cannot achieve goals and objectives if you are

26

as the fool in Proverbs 26:11 or slothful or lazy as the person in Proverbs 26:14, 20:4. Each and every one will be rewarded according to their works as stated in Revelation 20:12 and 22:12. Therefore we should not be fools or lazy, for II Thessalonians 3:10 states, For even when we were with you, this we commanded you, that if any would not work, neither should he eat. Therefore, we must also work to obtain our goals and objectives. We must acquire economic skills (not just degrees) by going to school and staying in school. The acquisition of such economic skills will enable us to produce quality products and services, and to obtain ownership and control of our own economic entities in our communities.

We have been given the secrets for success. All nations are blessed in Abraham, Genesis 18:8, 22:18, 26:4. Abraham, Isaac, and Jacob were very rich and wealthy, with silver and gold, cattle, oxen, assess, menservants, and maidservants. Your reward can also be great if you believe in God as they did and walk in the statutes of life without committing iniquities. We reap what we sow, Galatians 6:7.

You can acquire the wisdom, knowledge and understanding that you need, Proverbs 4:7. You may not receive it according to your timeline or my timeline, but it is on the main timeline. There is only one person that can give you the wisdom, knowledge and understanding that you need, Proverbs 2:6. You should know who to trust and what understanding you should not lean unto, Proverbs 3:5. You should go to the only one who can give you the wisdom, knowledge and understanding that you need, as man cannot give it to you. Man cannot be your mediator, I Timothy 2:5. Don't tarry too long with people or organizations stuck on foolishness. You must

27

be able to discern between the righteous and the wicked, Malachi 3:18. The wicked shall be destroyed, Psalms 37: and 73:. The hour of temptation shall come upon the whole world, to try them that dwell upon the earth. You choose the God whom you will serve.

Being blessed is a wonderful joy, a time to eat, drink and enjoy the good of all your labour. It even makes retirement so much better, as you can travel and enjoy the finer things in life. A good economic agenda will assure your path to economic autonomy. You will know to pray, work and study and acquire the economic skills (not just degrees) that will enable you to succeed, and to acquire ownership and control of economic assets. This also benefits the community and will help lift the community from the bottom of the economic ladder. The community will have an economic agenda and dollars are turned over in businesses in the community. Residents will feel better about their community and begin to exercise financial accountability with the proper internal controls in opening up other businesses in the community. You can be Prosperous and Healthy and not stuck in Poverty. Behold, we have been foretold all things. The WORD is TRUTH. Practice TRUTH, Teach TRUTH, Know The TRUTH !

Enter in by The Door; and Abide in The
True Vine (St. John 10:9, 15:1)

Seek Wisdom, Knowledge and Understanding
and Abide in The True Vine

The Vile One's A-Coming

In these dark and deep latter days the fourth beast arises from the sea, and it is more diverse from all the rest as seen by Daniel (Daniel 7:7, Revelation 13:1). Another beast also rises and comes in peaceably to deceive many. He appears to be the righteous one, but is indeed the vile one (anti Christ) Daniel 8:23-26, 9:26-27, 11:21-25, Revelation 13:11.

The vile one shall rise just as the prophet Daniel saw and at the appointed time; Daniel also saw the abomination of desolation standing where it ought not be (St. Matthew 24:15, St. Mark 13:14, St. Luke 21:20). We know that dark and terrible days are a-coming, and that of the armies that shall compass Jerusalem only the sixth part of them was left not slain (Ezekiel 38:-39:).

In these dark and terrible days we know that the fourth part of the earth will be killed with the sword, hunger, death, and the beasts of the earth (Revelation 6:8). We also know that when the 200 million man army is loosed, that the third part of men will be slain, killed by the fire, smoke and brimstone (Revelation 9:15-18).

The vile one knows that he has but a little while to tarry here on earth, and is dedicated to destroying many through peace, and enters peaceably (Daniel 8:23-26, 11:21-25). We know that he will enter into a peace agreement that will not last (Daniel 9:26-27).

The vile one's a-coming with an ulterior motive, and he can be transformed as an angel of light, and his ministers transformed as ministers of righteousness; whose end shall be according to their works (II Corinthians 11:14-

31

15). Power was given to him over all kindreds, and tongues, and nations (Revelation 13:7). "And all that dwell upon the earth shall worship him, whose names are not written in the book of life of the Lamb slain from the foundation of the world" (Revelation 13:8).

And he causeth all, both small and great, rich and poor, free and bond, to receive a mark in their right hand, or in their foreheads (Revelation 13:16). But we know who the locusts cannot hurt or torment (Revelation 9:4). We know that God's servants shall be sealed, for there was a great multitude, which no man could number, of all nations and kindreds, and peoples, and tongues, stood before the throne, and before the Lamb (Revelation 7:9). We know that these are they which came out of great tribulation, and have washed their robes, and made them white in the blood of the Lamb (Revelation 7:14).

We know that there will be a punishment of nations (Isaiah 45:7, 18:1, 28:, Amos 3:6, Daniel 9:11-14, Hosea 9:11, Joel 1:-3:, Amos 1:-9:, Revelation 18:). We also know that we shall all be rewarded according to our works (Psalm 62:12, St. Matthew 16:27, Revelation 20:12, 22:12).

Daniel saw a time of great trouble (Daniel 12:1, 10). But we know who can keep us from the hour of temptation that shall come upon all the world, to try them that dwell upon the earth (Revelation 3:10).

The Resurrection

The Preacher states that, "One generation passeth away, and another generation cometh: but the earth abideth forever", Ecclesiastes 1:4. All the rivers run into the sea; yet the sea is not full; unto the place from whence the rivers come, thither they return again, Ecclesiastes 1:7. In the sweat of thy face shalt thou eat bread, till thou return to the ground; for out of it wast thou taken: for dust thou art, and unto dust shalt thou return, Genesis 3:19. There is no resurrection of flesh and blood; but there is a Resurrection. The Old Testament Prophet Daniel tells us there is a Resurrection, Daniel 12:2. We are also told that there is a Resurrection in St. John 5:28-29, 11:23-26, Acts 24:15.

We come into this world born from our mother's womb. Then we are told that we must be born again to enter into the kingdom of God, St. John 3:3. We know that flesh and blood cannot inherit the kingdom of God, I Corinthians 15:50. We know that flesh and blood-dust returns to dust, as Ecclesiastes 12:7 states, "Then shall the dust return to the earth as it was: and the spirit shall return unto God who gave it". In II Corinthians 5:8 we are told to be absent from the body, is to be present with the Lord. There are celestial bodies, and bodies terrestrial, a natural body and a spiritual body; and **we shall all be changed at the last trump**, I Corinthians 15:35-58. There is a second coming, I Thessalonians 4:13-18, II Thessalonians 2:1-8, Revelation 1:7, 19:11-16, 20:5, St. Matthew 24:30, St. Mark 13:26, St. Luke 21:27. We have been foretold all things, St. Mark 13:23.

We have been told the way to everlasting life, St. John 14:6. We know that there is only one mediator between

God and men, I Timothy 2:5. The choice is ours, we can choose life or death; for the bells will toll and death will come for many. He that goeth down to the grave shall come up no more: He shall return no more to his house, Job 7:9-10. The body goes back to the dust of the ground, and the spirit back to God. When I return to my God I want to go to the good side of the great gulf fixed, St. Luke 16:26. Flesh and blood cannot inherit the kingdom of God. I want to be raised incorruptible in my celestial and spiritual body at the last trump when we are all changed. There is a Resurrection of the dead both the just and the unjust. Let no man deceive you.

Blessed and holy is he that hath part in the first resurrection, and we know who takes part in the first resurrection, Revelation 20:4-6. We know what happens in the millennium, Revelation 20:, and that we will recognize and can help certain relatives in the millennium, Ezekiel 44:25. We know when the Great White Throne Judgment occurs, Revelation 20:11; and who takes part in the second death, Revelation 20:13-15, 21:8. We know how we shall all be rewarded, Revelation 20:12, 22:12. Behold, We have been foretold all things.

Behold, We Have Been Foretold All Things

Marriage and Divorce

After a divorce, remarriage is not permitted as long as the ex spouse is alive. You must remain unmarried as long as the ex spouse liveth; or be reconciled to the ex spouse. **(I Corinthians 7:10,11,39 and Romans 7:2-3).**

To remarry while an ex spouse is alive is adultery. **(Romans 7:3, St. Matthew 19:9, St. Mark 10:11-12, St. Luke 16:18).**

Moses suffered the people (because of the hardness of their hearts) to put away their wives by giving them a writing of divorcement. But, Jesus said, "from the beginning it was not so". **(St. Matthew 19:7-8).**

Jesus said, "whosoever shall put away his wife, except it be for fornication, and shall marry another, committeth adultery: and whoso marrieth her which is put away doth commit adultery". **(St. Matthew 19:9).**

Male and female married are one flesh (no more twain) and what God has joined together, let no man put asunder. **(St. Matthew 19:3-9).**

An engaged (espoused) couple is referred to as husband and wife. **(St. Matthew 1:18-25 and St. Luke 1:27 & 2:5).** Fornication would occur during engagement period; after marriage it is adultery.

St. Mark 7:7 - "Howbeit in vain do they worship me, teaching for doctrines the commandments of men".

Deuteronomy 18:15-22 - "The Lord thy God will raise up unto thee a Prophet from the midst of thee, of thy brethren, like unto me; unto him ye shall hearken;"

Ask, Seek and Knock (St. Matthew 7:7)

WOMEN TEACHERS (Preachers)

I Timothy 2:10-14   - No women teachers; women keep silence in churches.

I Corinthians 14:34-35 - No women teachers; women keep silence in churches.

I Timothy 3:1-12   - Men are Bishops and deacons.

Galatians 1:8-9   - Preach one Gospel.

Ecclesiastes 7:26-28 - Woman not found (Proverbs 5:3-4).

Numbers 22:27-28   - (II Peter 2:15-16) Balaam's ass spoke with a man's voice - (false prophet). Revelation 2:14.

Joel 2:28   - Women prophesying – not preaching.

St. Mark 16:9-10   - Mary didn't preach.

Isaiah 3:12   - Women rule – cause thee to err.

Isaiah 9:16-17   - Leaders cause thee to err, and they are destroyed.

Revelation 2:20   - Jezebel's teaching condemned.

Titus 2:3-5	-	Older women are to teach young women certain things (I Corinthians 14:40).
Judges 4:-5:	-	Deborah, a prophetess, was a judge over Israel. Judges served one or more tribes of Israel. **Deborah was not a preacher.**
Ruth 1:-4:	-	Ruth a Moabitess (foreigner) was absorbed into Israelite life and history. Ruth married Boaz and became the great-grandmother of King David. (Boaz, Obed, Jesse, David). **Ruth was not a preacher.**

St. Mark 7:7 - "Howbeit in vain do they worship me, teaching for doctrines the commandments of men".

Deuteronomy 18:15-22 - "The Lord thy God will raise up unto thee a Prophet from the midst of thee, of thy brethren, like unto me; unto him ye shall hearken;"

Gay and Lesbian Lifestyles
Condemned By God's Principles

In the beginning God made them male and female, and only male and female can become one when joined together by God (St. Matthew 19:4-6). It is often said that God is love and that we should also love, but God is true love, not a perverted love. God's word is very specific in condemning unlawful sexual relations and conduct. The laws on personal conduct are specific and not ambiguous. Deuteronomy 4:24 and Hebrews 12:29 tell us that God is a consuming fire.

Leviticus Chapter 18 Covers unlawful sexual relations, and verse 22 states, **"Thou shalt not lie with mankind, as with womankind: it is abomination"**. Leviticus 20:13 is in agreement with this condemnation. Deuteronomy Chapter 22 also covers laws of sexual conduct. Men should not lust after men, one toward another, in **vile affections.** We should not dishonor our bodies or engage in vile affections or **perverted love**. Don't be without understanding; seek wisdom, knowledge, and understanding. Seek righteousness and follow God's principles, Romans 1:18-32.

In I Corinthians 6:9-10 the effeminate is listed as one of the groups that will not inherit the kingdom of God. It is clearly stated that the unrighteous shall not inherit the kingdom of God. Revelation 22:8 tells us who takes part in the second death. Revelation 22:7-14 tells you what you should do.

We are told to love one another, but this should be a true love and not a perverted love. For God's love is a true love and he told us to love in truth and in deed, and not to love in word and in tongue (I John 3:18).

God's laws do not sanction homosexual unions and same sex marriages. Such unions including domestic partners are condemned by God's laws. God gave specific and direct laws on marriage and divorce in I Corinthians 7:10-11, 39 and Romans 7:2-3. Marriage is a union when male and female are no more twain when joined together by God (St. Matthew 19:3-9). Also see I Corinthians 11:3,8-9.

There is Only One Way to Truth and Righteousness, and only One True Vine and door we can enter to be saved and find truth and get pasture, (St. John 10:9, 14:6, 15:1). We can all be clean through the word that has been spoken to us; but we must read and study the word of truth, (II Timothy 2:15, St. John 15:3). Let us not remain crying in the waters and wandering in the wilderness of poverty and ignorance, stuck in the mud pile hooked on untold mind twisters. We need only apply the scriptural solutions to our current problems, as there is nothing new under the sun.

Stuck in The Mud-Pile Trapped in a Quagmire of Drugs, Alcohol, and Untold Folly - (Apply Scriptural Solutions)

Many people all over the land have become disillusioned by circumstances that they have succumbed to. They seek escape with other mind-twisters and pseudo solutions and other illusionary crutches that they become even more victimized and stuck in situations that appear overwhelming. There is a **Scriptural Solution**. But you must be committed to change, you can't keep doing the same old things you've been doing for years and expect a better result. You can't keep hanging around with the same old foolish folks doing the same things in a foolish rut. A fool will not change (Proverbs 26:11).

God intended for his people to be prosperous and healthy (not strategically misadjusted to be happy in poverty, ignorance, and on the bottom). We have been given specific instructions on how to be the head and not the tail, how to be above, not beneath. But there is a condition precedent to receiving these blessings; that is, to **Abide By, Keep, and Do All the Commandments of God (Deuteronomy 28:1-14).**

There is only one way as stated in **St. John 14:6**, but many people keep trying to do it their way leaning unto their understanding, and they keep slipping deeper in the mud-pile. There may be a temptation to jump in and try to save them, but don't jump in the mud-pile to try to save someone. Throw them a safety line and see if they're willing to take action to help lift them up and out of danger. Unless they're willing to change directions in life, they will linger in the mud-pile. They must know who they are, a knowledge of themselves, for there is only one way as stated in **St. John 14:6.**

But some will continue to try and do it their way using pig-feet logic or some kind of economic foolishness. Some will continue to party starting on Friday night into the Sabbath even waking up with a hangover polluting the Sabbath, even going back for more on Saturday night and getting up on Sunday morning going to worship; still not realizing why they are stuck on the bottom. We can have life and have life more abundantly as stated in **St. John 10:10** if we apply **Scriptural Solutions.** So let us get to the conclusion of the whole matter as stated in **Ecclesiastes 12:13-14.**

Scriptural Solutions – There are many religious institutions and places of worship in the community, and many of them are fragmentized by different denominations, doctrines and philosophies (denominations are not biblical). As Jesus stated in **St. Mark 7:7,** "Howbeit in vain do they worship me, teaching for doctrines the commandments of men". Therefore it is imperative that you find yourself a good bible teaching place of worship, for some are filled with false teachings. **Deuteronomy 18:15-22** tells you how to identify your true prophet. We must **Practice Truth, Teach Truth and Know The Truth**. We must be born again as stated in **St. John 3:3**, and be doers of the word, **I Peter 1:23**. We need not remain in poverty and ignorance or stuck in the mud-pile, for we know the way out as stated in **St. John 14:6**. There is only one mediator between God and men, **I Timothy 2:5**. But we must be committed to change, for to continue to proceed in a non-pragmatic direction will not give you a better result. Your environment must change and you must avoid negative influences and bad associations, or you will never apply scriptural solutions. You will continue to slumber around and have nothing and beg in harvest, **Proverbs 20:4 and 26:14.**

We can be prosperous and healthy and have life more abundantly, **Leviticus 11:, Deuteronomy 8:, Proverbs 28:19, St. John 10:10**. And also that every man should eat and drink, and enjoy the good of all his labour, it is the gift of God, **Ecclesiastes 3:13**. Each and every one of us must choose the direction we will take, but we shall all be rewarded according to our works; and we will only reap what we have sown, **Galatians 6:7.**

POVERTY - There is A Way Out!

To remain in poverty is contrary to God's word. (The destruction of the poor is their poverty. – Proverbs 10:15). God's people can be the head and not the tail, above and not beneath; But you must observe and do all the commandments of the Lord thy God: - Deuteronomy 28:13. All nations are blessed in Abraham (if you keep the covenant and observe and do all his commandments). Abraham, Isaac and Jacob were very prosperous and wealthy, they had silver and gold, cattle, oxen, asses, menservants, maidservants, land: - Deuteronomy 18:18, 22:18, 26:4, 13:2, 30:43.

Proverbs 10:15 - The rich man's wealth is his strong
city: the destruction of the poor
is their poverty.

Proverbs 20:13 - Love not sleep, lest thou come to
poverty; open thine eyes, and
thou shalt be satisfied with bread.

Proverbs 20:4 - The sluggard will not plow by
reason of the cold; therefore
shall he beg in harvest and have
nothing.

Proverbs 12:11 - He that tilleth his land shall be
satisfied with bread: but he that
followeth vain persons is void of
understanding.

Proverbs 28:19 - He that tilleth his land shall have plenty of bread: but he that followeth after vain persons shall have poverty enough.

Proverbs 26:11 - As a dog returneth to his vomit, so a Fool returneth to his folly.

Proverbs 26:14 - As the door turneth upon his hinges, so doth the slothful upon his bed.

Proverbs 13:18 - Poverty and shame shall be to him that refuseth instruction: but he that regardeth reproof shall be honored.

Proverbs 23:21 - For the drunkard and the glutton shall come to poverty: and drowsiness shall clothe a man with rags.

II Thessalonians 3:10 – For even when we were with you, this we commanded you, that if any would not work, neither should he eat. (James 2:17-26, Psalm 62:12, Revelation 20:12 & 22:12)

Proverbs 13:11 - Wealth gotten by vanity shall be diminished: but he that gathereth by labour shall increase.

Ecclesiastes 3:13 - And also that every man should eat and drink, and enjoy the good of all his labour, it is the gift of God.

Job 36:11 - If they obey and serve him, they shall spend their days in prosperity, and their years in pleasure.

St. John 10:10 - The thief cometh not, but for to steal, and to kill, and to destroy: I am come that they might have life, and that they might have it more abundantly.

St. John 14:6 - Jesus saith unto him, I am the way, the truth, and the life: no man cometh unto the Father, but by me.

I Timothy 2:5 - For there is one God, and one mediator between God and men, the man Christ Jesus.

St. John 3:3 - Jesus answered and said unto him, verily, verily, I say unto thee, except a man be born again, he cannot see the kingdom of God. (I Peter 1:23)

47

Blessings of Obedience -

Deuteronomy 28:1-14   Blessings of Obedience

Deuteronomy 28:1 -   And it shall come to pass, if
thou shalt hearken diligently
unto the voice of the Lord thy
God, to observe and to do all
his commandments which I
command thee this day, that the
Lord thy God will set thee on
high above all nations of the
earth:

Deuteronomy 28:2   - And all these blessings shall
come on thee, and overtake thee,
if thou shalt hearken unto the
voice of the Lord thy God.

Deuteronomy 28:13 - And the Lord shall make thee the
head, and not the tail; and
thou shalt be above only, and
thou shalt not be beneath; if that
thou hearken unto the
commandments of the Lord thy
God, which I command thee this
day, to observe and to do them.

Curses of Disobedience -
Deuteronomy 28:15-68

Ecclesiastes 12:13   - Let us hear the conclusion of
the whole matter: Fear God, and
keep his commandments: for
this is the whole duty of man.

We may have come from deep and humble
beginnings, but our One True Most High God
can bring us out of poverty

We can be the head and not the tail, above and not beneath; if we hearken to the commandments, observe and do them!

Let us also not defile our bodies with the unclean – Leviticus 11:44

Clean and Unclean Animals
(Leviticus Chapter 11 and Deuteronomy Chapter 14)

We have been given specific instructions on what to eat and what not to eat. We are supposed to be holy and not defile the body.

Whatsoever <u>parteth the hoof,</u> and is <u>clovenfooted,</u> and <u>cheweth the cud,</u> among the beasts, <u>that shall ye eat.</u> (Leviticus 11:3)

Nevertheless **these shall ye not eat** of them that chew the cud, or of them that divide the hoof: as the **camel,** because he cheweth the cud, but divideth not the hoof; he is unclean to you. (Leviticus 11:4)

And the **coney,** because he cheweth the cud, but divideth not the hoof; he is unclean unto you. (Leviticus 11:5)

And the **hare,** because he cheweth the cud, but divideth not the hoof; he is unclean unto you. (Leviticus 11:6)

And the **swine,** though he divide the hoof, and be clovenfooted, yet he cheweth not the cud; he is unclean to you. (Leviticus 11:7)

Of their flesh shall ye not eat, and their carcase shall ye not touch; they are unclean to you. (Leviticus 11:8)

<u>These shall ye eat</u> of all that are in the waters: <u>whatsoever hath fins and scales</u> in the waters, in the seas, and in the rivers, them shall ye eat. (Leviticus 11:9)

And all that have not fins and scales in the seas, and in the rivers, of all that move in the waters, and of any

51

living thing that is in the waters, they **shall be an abomination** unto you: (Leviticus 11:10)

They shall be even an abomination unto you; ye shall not eat of their flesh, but ye shall have their carcases in abomination. (Leviticus 11:11)

Whatsoever hath no fins nor scales in the waters, that **shall be an abomination** unto you. (Leviticus 11:12)

And these are they which ye shall have in abomination among the fowls; **they shall not be eaten,** they are an abomination: the **eagle**, and the **ossifrage**, and the **ospray**, (Leviticus 11:13)

And the **vulture**, and the **kite after his kind**; (Leviticus 11:14)

Every **raven after his kind**; (Leviticus 11:15)

And the **owl**, and the **night hawk**, and the **cuckoo**, and the **hawk after his kind**, (Leviticus 11:16)

And the **little owl**, and the **cormorant**, and the **great owl**, (Leviticus 11:17)

And the **swan**, and the **pelican**, and the **gier eagle**, (Leviticus 11:18)

And the **stork**, the **heron after her kind**, and the **lapwing**, and the **bat**. (Leviticus 11:19)

All fowls that creep, going upon all four, shall be **an abomination** unto you. (Leviticus 11:20)

Yet <u>these may ye eat</u> of <u>every flying creeping thing</u> that

goeth upon all four, which have legs above their feet, to leap withal upon the earth; (Leviticus 11:21)
Even these of them ye may eat; the locust after his kind, and the beetle after his kind, and the grasshopper after his kind. (Leviticus 11:22)

But **all other flying creeping things**, which have **four feet**, shall be **an abomination** unto you. (Leviticus 11:23)

And for these ye shall be unclean: whosoever toucheth the carcase of them shall be unclean until the even. (Leviticus 11:24)

And whosoever beareth aught of the carcase of them shall wash his clothes, and be unclean until the even. (Leviticus 11:25)

The carcases of every beast which **divideth the hoof**, and is **not clovenfooted, nor cheweth the cud, are unclean** unto you: every one that toucheth them shall be unclean. (Leviticus 11:26)

And **whatsoever goeth upon his paws**, among all manner of beasts that go on all four, those are **unclean** unto you: whoso toucheth their carcase shall be unclean until the even. (Leviticus 11:27)

And he that beareth the carcase of them shall wash his clothes, and be unclean until the even: they are unclean unto you. (Leviticus 11:28)

These also shall be **unclean** unto you among the creeping things that creep upon the earth; the **weasel**, and the **mouse**, and the **tortoise after his kind**, (Leviticus 11:29)

And the **ferret**, and the **chameleon**, and the **lizard**, and the **snail**, and the **mole**. (Leviticus 11:30)

These are unclean to you among all that creep: whosoever doth touch them, when they be dead, shall be unclean until the even. (Leviticus 11:31)

And **every creeping thing that creepeth** upon the earth shall be an abomination; it **shall not be eaten**. (Leviticus 11:41)

Whatsoever goeth upon the belly, and whatsoever goeth **upon all four**, or whatsoever **hath more feet among all creeping things** that creep upon the earth, **them shall ye not eat**; for they are an abomination. (Leviticus 11:42)

Ye shall not make yourselves abominable with any creeping thing that creepeth, neither shall ye make **yourselves unclean** with them, that ye should **be defiled** thereby. (Leviticus 11:43)

For I am the Lord your God: ye shall therefore **sanctify** yourselves, and ye shall **be holy**; for **I am holy**: **neither shall ye defile yourselves** with any manner of creeping thing that creepeth upon the earth. (Leviticus 11:44)

For I am the Lord that bringeth you up out of the land of Egypt, to be your God: ye shall therefore **be holy, for I am holy**. (Leviticus 11:45)

Thou shalt not eat any abominable thing. (Deuteronomy 14:3)

These are the beasts which ye shall eat: the ox, the sheep, and the goat. (Deuteronomy 14:4)

The hart, and the roebuck, and the fallow deer, and the wild goat, and the pygarg, and the wild ox, and the chamois. (Deuteronomy 14:5)

And every beast that parteth the hoof, and cleaveth the cleft into two claws, and cheweth the cud among the beasts, that ye shall eat. (Deuteronomy 14:6)

Nevertheless these **ye shall not eat** of them that chew the cud, or of them that divide the cloven hoof; as the **camel**, and the **hare**, and the **coney**: for they chew the cud, but divide not the hoof; therefore they are **unclean unto you**. (Deuteronomy 14:7)

And the **swine**, because it divideth the hoof, yet cheweth not the cud, **it is unclean** unto you: ye shall not eat of their flesh, nor touch their dead carcase. (Deuteronomy 14:8)

As we sojourn here in this land on our journey home, we may come across obstacles placed in our way. But the Day of the Lord shall come; we can be saved even though some may still be wandering in the wilderness of hopelessness, going down that long road that leads to nowhere fast. Let us get a renewed spirit of the mind, put on the new man and move on.

WHERE IS THAT LAND?

Where is that land that is shadowing with wings? – Isaiah 18:

Where is that land of the drunkards of Ephraim? – Isaiah 28:

Where is that land where they have erred through strong drink, and stumble in judgment? – Isaiah 28:7.

Where is that land and what happens to the glory of Ephraim? – Hosea 9:11.

Where is that land and where is the vision about that land? – Jeremiah 50:

Where is that land where my people hath been lost sheep: their shepherds have caused them to go astray? – Jeremiah 50:7.

Where is that land and what is the vision in the midst of that land? – Jeremiah 51:

Where is that land that the prophet unto the nations wrote about? – Jeremiah 51:60,64.

Where is that land that is to become fallen and desolate? – Revelation 18:

Where is that land that is become the habitation of devils, and the hold of every foul spirit, and a cage of every unclean and hateful bird? – Revelation 18:2.

Where is that land and who hath remembered her iniquities? - Revelation 18:5.

Where is that land where in one hour her judgment is come? - Revelation 18:10,17,19.

Where is that land that in her was found the blood of prophets, and of saints, and of all that were slain upon the earth? – Revelation 18:24.

Where is that land? Open thine eyes and flee out of the midst of her!

THE DAY OF THE LORD

BEHOLD, We have been foretold All Things. (St. Matthew 24:25, St. Mark 13:23, Amos 3:7)

The Day of the Lord is a day of destruction, darkness and gloominess, clouds and thick darkness, great and very terrible, darkness and not light, very dark, and no brightness in it. (Joel 1:15, 2:1, 2, 10, 11, 30, 31, 3:15, Amos 5:18, 20, Obadiah 1:15)

We know that Jerusalem will be compassed with armies (St. Luke 21:20). We know that many false prophets shall arise and deceive many (St. Matthew 24:11,24,5, St. Mark 13:6,20, St. Luke 21:8, Jeremiah 10:21, 14:14, 23:1, Ezekiel 13: & 34:, II Peter 2:, II Corinthians 11:13-15, Isaiah 56:10,11, St. Matthew 15:14)

We have been given the Prophecy against Gog **(Ezekiel 38: & 39:)** and we know that in the latter years that out of the north parts that Gog will lead the armies that come against Israel. Gog, the chief prince of Meshech and Tubal, and with them will be Persia, Ethiopia, and Libya. God said I will turn thee back and leave but the sixth part of thee. Thou shalt fall upon the open mountains of Israel. Thou shalt fall upon the open field. But ye shall be rained upon with an overflowing rain, and great hailstones, fire and brimstone. And God will send a fire on Magog, and among them that dwell carelessly in the isles. (Magog-Gog is Russia: - Magog, Meshech, and Tubal are sons of Japheth and Japheth is the son of Noah, Genesis 10:) **Zechariah 14:12** describes the plague wherewith the Lord will smite all the people that have fought against Jerusalem; Their flesh shall consume away while they stand upon their feet, and their eyes shall consume away in their holes, and their tongue shall consume away in their mouth.

Behold, we have been foretold all things, and we know that terrible times are coming. Revelation gives us the Seven Seals and we know that the seals will be opened and we know what will happen when each seal is opened. In Revelation 6:8 the fourth seal is opened and we know that Death sits upon that pale horse, and that power was given to them over the **fourth part of the earth**, to kill with sword, and with hunger, and with death, and with the beasts of the earth.

Revelation 8: tells us that the seventh seal is opened (seven angels with seven trumpets) and that each angel will sound. In Revelation 9: we know that the fifth angel sounds and we are told what hurts men five months (Revelation 9:1-10) In Revelation 9:13-18 the sixth angel sounds (7th seal 6th trump) and that **the third part of men are slain** by, fire, smoke, and brimstone. And the number of the army of the horsemen were two hundred thousand thousand.

We know that we shall not all sleep, but we shall all be changed, in a moment, in the twinkling of an eye, at the last trump. I Corinthians 15:51, 52.

We know that the **hour of temptation** shall come upon all the world, to try them that dwell upon the earth. Revelation 3:10 tells us who can save us from that hour. Revelation 3:7 lets us know that we can rely on, he that openeth, and no man shutteth; and shutteth, and no man openeth. Revelation 3:20 lets us know that someone is standing at the door knocking, and we should open the door.

II Timothy 3:16 tells us that, "All scripture is given by inspiration of God, and is profitable for doctrine, for reproof, for correction, for instruction in righteousness". II Peter 1:21 tells us that, prophecy came not in old time by the will of man: but holy men of God spake as they were moved by the Holy Spirit.

Souls Yonder

Saved but Still Wandering in the Wilderness

We are all saved by grace through faith, and not by the things in our perspective which we do or pretend to do. We know that faith without works is dead, and we shall all be rewarded according to our works, therefore we all should study and Work! (Ephesians 2:8, James 2:17-26, I Thessalonians 4:11, II Thessalonians 3:6-12, Psalm 62:12, Revelation 20:12, 22:12). We are all supposed to be and can be the children of the "Most High God" if we would only Observe and Do his Commandments, Statutes and Laws as we were commanded to do. If we do we can all be partakers of the covenant and receive the "Blessings of Obedience" of the "Word of Truth". There are rewards and blessings for obedience to the word of God, just as they are recorded in the "Word of Truth" (Deuteronomy 28:13). We all have free will and can choose the direction in which we want to go. But if we choose the wrong direction we will continue to wander in the wilderness even though you may be saved in your own eyes.

The children of Israel were saved and led out of bondage in Egypt, and crossed the Red Sea and knew that the Promised Land awaited them. Yet they were saved from their previous fate in bondage, but were left to wander in the wilderness for forty years. They were saved by Grace, but still chose to worship false gods and not hearken to their true God that brought them out of bondage and fed them in the wilderness. So they remained there in the wilderness until the unfaithful generation died out, as they had their same old mindset and had not put on the new man renewed in knowledge, a renewed spirit of the mind (Ephesians 4:23-24, Colossians 3:10).

The same is true today as some people have been saved by Grace, yet they continue to wander in the Wilderness of Poverty and Ignorance, drugs and other untold mind twisters. They create or perpetuate their problems and then try to turn the problem over to God to resolve. But that is just like praying for the impossible. For we have been told what to do and what not to do, we know whose Commandments, Statutes and Laws we should obey. Yet some are still trying to do it their way and wondering why they remain stuck in the mud pile in poverty and laden in deep debt on the bottom of the economic ladder. A "new mindset" comes when you are "born again", by the "Word of Truth" (I Peter 1:23-25). God did not intend for his people to remain in poverty and deep debt wandering in the wilderness of crime ridden neighborhoods over run with thugs, drugs and other untold mind twisters.

We have been given the Authority and Responsibility to resolve certain problems and have been shown and given the way. We cannot create or perpetuate our problems and then pray for a panacea; that's an impossible prayer. We have free will and can choose whom we will serve, or we can do it our way and say we are saved by grace, but still remain wandering in the wilderness. We can be the head and not the tail, above and not beneath, but we must fulfill the condition precedent as stated in Deuteronomy 28:13. For there is only one way (St. John 14:6). Behold (St. Mark 13:23).

The Road That Leads to Nowhere Fast

In our sojourn here in the flesh as we walk under the sun and our life is as a shadow on the long road home. There is also a road of life that can lead to nowhere fast if one continues on and remains in such an untold direction. That in itself should not be surprising, but it is somewhat shocking that so many people are marching down the road going nowhere fast. It's like they're marching to catch up to their image in the mirror held by the foolish folks leading them astray. There are vain persons out there leading them astray all up and down the boulevard and all over our economically depressed neighborhoods. I would often stand at the corner of my front porch in the city and watch them roam while tripping on untold mind-twisters and other vices.

Some may be looking for rides to the other side of town. Ask me for a ride and I have a three prong test that you must pass before you can ride with me in my ride. You must be at least 18 ½ years old, you must have a 3.5 and you must be a Doer. Many keep on just a-marching down the road giving high fives and talking jive. It's like they're not even alive, not even aware, with no cares, just marching on down the road that leads to nowhere. I just keep looking at them while passing them by. They just keep giving each other high fives. Again they ask me for a ride, and I ask them if they have a 3.5; and then they finally ask, what's a 3.5?

I pause and look up and down the road from my safe vantage point. I always make sure before I speak and act and end up in the joint. And then I answer, a 3.5 is a desired G.P.A. of 3.5, and you'll need a 3.5 to ride with me in my fine ride!

So now let's go back to step one (1) and get some things done. First you'll need to acquire some Economic Skills. Get off that Road to Nowhere and shed those illiterate ills. To remain on the Road to Nowhere will only lead to even more poverty and ignorance in these already overloaded economically depressed neighborhoods.

We can all get off that Road to Nowhere, as we all have "Free Will". The choice is yours, and you can get off that road to illiterate ills. Study and Work! Study and Work! (I Thessalonians 4:11). Not only will you acquire some **Economic Skills** and expertise; you'll end up with a 3.5 and get to ride with me in my fine ride. Take Action and be a Doer!

My ride is the right ride and I'm not driving down that Road That Leads to Nowhere Fast. I prefer Economic Skills over Illiterate Ills. So come on and let's all take the Right Road!

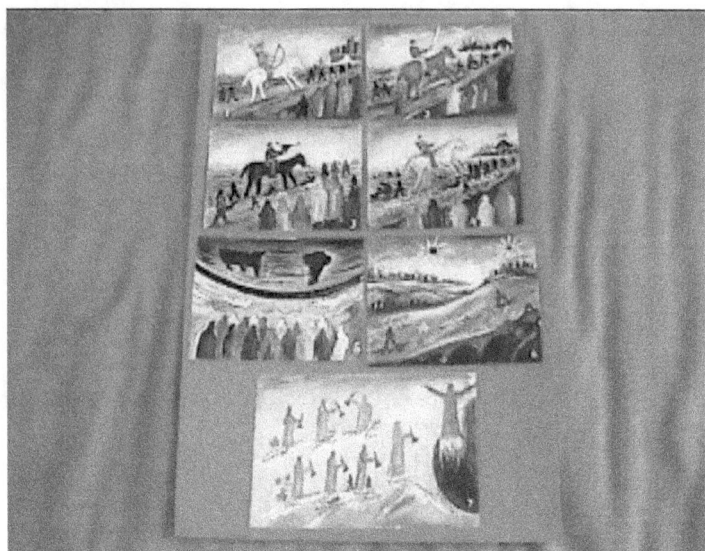

The Seven Seals

64

A Renewed Spirit of the Mind

As long as a man continues to look at things the same old way, he will continue to see what he sees through the same old mindset. This will only keep him where he is with the old mind no matter how young or old he is.

One must look through the thick dark clouds and see the vision of the "new man" with a new mindset. There is a process for the "liberation of the mind" with a new thought process. But as long as you continue in the ways of the world there will be no "renewed spirit of the mind". There is "only one way" (St. John 14:6). We must put on the new man with a new mindset and a new vision (Ephesians 4:23-24). We need not remain in poverty and on the bottom of the economic ladder crammed into high crime and drug laden poverty pocket communities called public housing projects.

Families in such communities must band together and acquire their own houses on their own properties, and this is possible with a renewed spirit of the mind. You cannot rely on public housing authorities to provide permanent housing for you forever. Hurricane Katrina's aftermath has taught us this very clearly. Many such public housing authorities are in effect bankrupt. We need not remain in poverty (Proverbs 28:19, 12:11). The destruction of the poor is their poverty (Proverbs 10:15). We must Study and Work (I Thessalonians 4:11, II Thessalonians 3:6-12).

No one will give us a home, we must work for what we get, as we will all reap what we have sown (Galatians 6:7). We must plow and plant to have a good harvest (Proverbs 20:4). We are all rewarded according to our

65

works (Psalm 62:12, Revelation 20:12, 22:12). The new man must be renewed in knowledge (Colossians 3:10).

The economic struggles of our prior generations have taught us many lessons that we should heed. They maintained the fortitude and discipline to succeed with a vision under seemingly insurmountable obstacles. And now we must continue to Study and Work to make it even better for all those who will follow; we must all be prepared for there is no free ride.

Let us listen and take heed, and not be left Crying in the Waters.

The Economic Struggles of My Prior Two Generations

1. Where were my parents born and raised?
2. What type of schools did they attend?
3. What type of shelter did their families have?
4. What type of jobs did their parents have?
5. How did they survive economically, and what were some of the hardships that they had to endure?
6. What type of educational opportunities did they have?
7. What type of economic opportunities did they have?
8. What type of work experiences did they have?
9. What type of job skills did they have?
10. Did they become self sufficient and independent?
11. How did my parents provide for their children?
12. What type of educational opportunities did their children (me) have?
13. What type of economic opportunities did their children (me) have?
14. How did my parents acquire their house?
15. What type of work experiences did my parents have?
16. What type of job skills did my parents acquire?

We do not have the type of economic struggles to endure that our prior generations had to endure! Therefore, you can obtain a "new mindset" and acquire the necessary skills to succeed! Study and Work!

Children Need and Must Have DCTTV
(Discipline – Correction – Training – Teaching – Vision)

Children need and must have DCTTV, Proverbs 22:6, 15 and 22:17, 18. Parents have been given the authority and responsibility to give their children DCTTV. Yet too many parents seem to perpetuate their children's problems and expect others to solve the problems for them. Some of the parents even turn over the problems to God, yet they still continue to perpetuate the problem. Some people have good intentions and want to be a part of the panacea not realizing that they themselves are a major part of the problem.

Parents were given the authority and responsibility to raise up a child in the way he should go, and when he is old he will not depart from it (Proverbs 22:6). Parents are also expected to correct their children as it is the rod of correction that drives foolishness far from them (Proverbs 22:15). Parents must teach their children and give them a vision of what they can become if they do the right thing (Proverbs 29:17-18). Parents are expected to discipline, correct, train, teach and give their children a vision with goals and objectives so that they can become focused and set on becoming productive. Discipline is a branch of learning and children will not be able to learn and be obedient to laws, etc. if they are not taught discipline at home. The schools will only return to you what you sent to them, and if you send the schools a child with no discipline, then the only thing the schools can return to you is your child with no discipline. The children with no discipline usually end up dropping out and hanging out.

68

Some parents complain that they can't get their children to do certain things, yet these same parents let their children bring their pernicious nonsense into their homes. Parents let their boomerang nation children live in their house under the children's rules; this is a classic example of how the parent's actions or inactions keep perpetuating the problems. The parents are thereby accessories three times, before the fact, during the act, and after the fact!

A child without DCTTV is like being Saved but still wandering in the wilderness of poverty and ignorance, stuck in the mud pile on the bottom of the economic ladder. The children of Israel were saved from bondage, but wandered in the wilderness for forty years. Some people find themselves still wandering in the wilderness of drugs and other untold mind twisters with the same old mind. The new man must be renewed in the spirit of his mind (Ephesians 4:23, 24). The old man must pass away and the new man emerges with a new mindset; born again from above by the Word of Truth (I Peter 1:23-25). Renewed in knowledge pursuant to (Colossians 3:10).

There is Only One Way (St. John 14:6). We were given specific instructions on why we should Observe and Do All the Commandments and Statutes. You can't turn over a problem to God if you are still perpetuating the problem and God gave you the authority and responsibility to solve and take care of the problem. Quit trying to do it your way. You must do what God told you to do (Deuteronomy 8:1-3, 28:1-2, 13, Ecclesiastes 12:13).

Get up and get with it, you are wise; Study and Work (I Thessalonians 4:11, II Thessalonians 3:6-12), and make sure you've got your DCTTV!

Continue to Seek Knowledge

Study and Work! Study and Work!
(As We Were Commanded To)

We were commanded to Study and Work! Study and Work! So what is the problem? We can all be saved and still remain on the bottom of the economic ladder, because each and every one of us will be rewarded according to our works. (II Timothy 2:15, I Thessalonians 4:11, II Thessalonians 3:10-12, Psalm 62:12, St. Matthew 16:27, Revelation 20:12, 2:12). And faith without works is dead (James 2:17-26). To be hearers of the word and not doers of the word is to deceive oneself (James 1:22-27).

Able bodied people should be productive, and not foolish and unprofitable as described in St. Matthew Chapter 25:. Able bodied people should not remain in poverty on the bottom of the economic ladder, for it is written that "the destruction of the poor is their poverty" (Proverbs 10:15). It is also written that "the man that tilleth his land shall have plenty of bread", to remain in poverty means that you are following the wrong people and you are void of understanding (Proverbs 28:19, 12:11).

We must Study and Work! Study and Work! And identify and work the Major Problems in our communities, otherwise our communities will remain economically depressed. Some of the Major Problems are:

- High rate of poverty and illiteracy
- High drop out rate
- High crime rate
- High rate of illegitimate births
- High rate of unskilled workers

71

The people in the affected communities are the only one's that can set the priorities and establish a modus operandi that can make the identification and working of the issues successful. They must stand up and take action, and do what they know should be done to stabilize our communities. The destruction of the poor is their poverty, and we need not remain in poverty when we can be the head and not the tail (Deuteronomy 28:13) if we fulfill the condition precedent stated therein.

We should love our neighbour, but everyone is not your neighbour (St. Luke 10:29-37). You cannot trust everyone and everyone in the city village cannot raise a child. We can all be saved and still remain on the bottom of the economic ladder, the choice is ours as we have our own free will.

Now stop, and listen, and let us get to the conclusion of the whole matter (Ecclesiastes 12:13)

There is No Free Ride

We Have Much To Do,
and a Long Way To Go, and
There Is No Free Ride!
If Each One Does a Little; Together,
We Can Accomplish A Lot,
Injustices May Linger . . . But,
We Must Move On and Succeed in Spite of Obstacles!
Because,
We Have Much To Do,
and a Long Way To Go, and
There Is No Free Ride!

Don't Practice Economic Foolishness,
Stay in School and Get a Skill, and Be Prepared to
Compete in the Global Economic Arena!   Have an
Economic Agenda!
No Economic Agenda, No Economic Autonomy.

We Have Much To Do, and a Long Way To Go, and
There is No Free Ride!

"You Can be The Head, and Not the Tail" (as stated in
Deuteronomy 28:13).
But, only "If" you fulfill the condition precedent stated
in Deuteronomy 28:13. Think and Act!

Study and Work – Acquire Land, and Develop your
Land and Obtain Economic Autonomy. (Proverbs 28:19,
12:11)

No One is Coming to Help or Save Foolish or Lazy
People. (Proverbs 26:11, 26:14, 20:4, 10:15).

Stop, and Listen . . .
Right Now;
"Let us get to the Conclusion of the Whole Matter" (as stated in Ecclesiastes 12:13).

There is Only One Way

Let Us Judge Not Any Man
But All Are Not The Same – Some Are Non-Productive

Let us judge not any man, for there is only one judge. But every tree is known by its own fruit (St. Luke 6:). Some people are wise and some people are foolish (St. Matthew 25:1-13, Proverbs 26:11). Some people are productive and some people are non productive (St. Matthew 25:13-30), they are unprofitable (St. Matthew 25:30).

Some people are the head and some people are the tail (Deuteronomy 28:13, 44). Some people till their own land and have plenty of bread (Proverbs 28:19). But some people are as sluggards (Proverbs 20:4, 26:14). Some able-bodied people refuse to work and eat their own bread (II Thessalonians 3:10-12), to remain in poverty is destruction (Proverbs 10:15). There is value and reward in study and work, and faith without works is dead (II Timothy 2:15, James 2:17-26).

Some are productive, some are not; some are the head, and some are the tail, some are law a-biding and some are not. Stop, think and use your free will and choose the way in which you will go. But, Remember "There is Only One Way" (St. John 14:6).

We are not all the same; some choose to stay in school and acquire Economic Skills. Some choose to drop out and hang out with others with no economic skills going nowhere fast. If you hang out with non-productive people, you'll end up going in the same direction they are going.

Some people Teach The Truth, Practice Truth, and Know The Truth. Others end up hooked on untold mind twisters just roaming all over going nowhere fast. They just bounce around all up and down the boulevard partying and dancing with the Devil in the Devil's Den, and the den's on fire.

As we all come to that critical crossroad in our journey; we must decide the way and direction we will take. But remember, "There is Only One Way". I intend to remain in my booth and do the right thing. If you do not intend to be productive, you cannot sit with me in my booth, and we cannot be associates. I intend to Practice Truth, Teach Truth, and Know The Truth!

We judge not any man; but, you must be able "to discern the righteous from the wicked, from him that serveth God, and from him that serveth him not" (Malachi 3:18).

For we shall all be rewarded according to our works (Psalm 62:12, St. Matthew 16:27, Revelation 20:12, 22:12).

Now, let us get to the conclusion of the whole matter and do our duty (Ecclesiastes 12:13). For we shall all reap what we have sown (Galatians 6:7).

Behold, we have been foretold all things (St. Mark 13:23, St. Matthew 24:25).

Crying in the Waters

There is a cry in the night and beyond, of people hurting, as the river is rising, and a new day a-dawning. The cries are louder now and oh so near, of so many people hurting in the waters. No one has come to help them in their hour of need as they are walking in the waters. Who will come to help them in their greatest hour of need?

Gather the people together, men, and women, and children, and thy stranger that is within thy gates, that they may hear, and that they may learn, and fear the Lord your God, and observe to do all the words of this law: (Deuteronomy 31:12)

What happens in that day when God hides his face from them; shall they be devoured, and many evils and troubles befall them; (Deuteronomy 31:17, 18, 21, 29). Listen to The Song of Moses (Deuteronomy 32:) and you will know who to ask, and who will be provoked to anger with a foolish nation.

There are cries all over the land as people are hurting from sea to sea and beyond. Why is all this evil among the people, and who brought this evil upon the people? (Daniel 9:11-14, Isaiah 45:7, Amos 3:6)

We know what happens to the glory of Ephraim (Hosea 9:11). We know that dark and terrible days are a-coming (Revelation 6:8, 9:15). We know who the king of the tormenters is (Revelation 9:11). We also know who shall not be hurt (Revelation 9:4).

We know that we have the covenant and who wrote the covenant (Genesis 9:11, Deuteronomy 9:10-11). We know that we can be the head and not the tail, if we only fulfill the condition precedent (Deuteronomy 28:13).

We know that we have God's righteousness and mercy (Romans 9:11-18). We know that Christ is our High Priest (Hebrews 9:11). We know who is everlasting and who is Alpha and Omega (Psalm 90:2, Revelation 1:8). We know who is the only one that can keep us from the hour of temptation, which shall come upon all the world, to try them that dwell upon the earth (Revelation 3:10). We know who stands at the door knocking and what we should do (Revelation 3:20).

We know that the prophet Daniel looked and he saw the abomination of desolation standing where it ought not be (St. Matthew 24:15, St. Mark 13:14, St. Luke 21:20). This will occur here on earth in the latter days.

We know that the race is not to the swift, nor the battle to the strong, . . . but time and chance happeneth to them all (Ecclesiastes 9:11). Now stop; Let us hear the conclusion of the whole matter: (Ecclesiastes 12:13).

A man must come out of darkness, and find his way into the light; but if he relies on himself to find his way out he may linger forever in his darkness. There is only one way (St. John 14:6). There is only one mediator between God and men (I Timothy 2:5).

Behold, we have been foretold all things (St. Matthew 24:25, St. Mark 13:23).

Behold, Behold

Giving Thanks Always

Prayers of Thanks

Our Heavenly Father we Thank Thee for this food. Feed all our faithful fellowservants all over the land as you are feeding us, for Jesus sake, Amen.

Our Heavenly Father we Thank Thee for this food. We Thank Thee for our health and strength, so that we may till our land and have plenty of bread, as stated in Proverbs 28:19. Grant your wisdom, knowledge and understanding to all our faithful fellowservants so that they may be fed, as you are feeding us. This we ask in Jesus name, Amen.

Our Heavenly Father we Thank Thee for this food. We Thank Thee for your wisdom, knowledge and understanding in Proverbs 28:19, which states that; the man that tilleth his land shall have plenty of bread, but he that followeth after vain persons shall have poverty enough. Grant your wisdom, knowledge and understanding to all our faithful fellowservants so that they may be fed, as you are feeding us. This we ask in Jesus name, Amen.

Our Heavenly Father we Thank Thee for this food. We Thank Thee for our health and strength. We Thank Thee for not being like those who refuse to work and should not eat, as stated in II Thessalonians 3:10. Grant your wisdom, knowledge and understanding to all our faithful fellowservants so that they may be fed, as you are feeding us. This we ask in Jesus name, Amen.

The 12 Tribes of Israel (Jacob)

Reuben   -   (Leah)
Simeon   -   "
Levi   -   "
Judah   -   "
Dan   -   (Bilhah-Rachel's Handmaid)
Naphtali -   "   "   "
Gad   -   (Zilpah-Leah's Handmaid)
Asher   -   "   "   "
Issachar -   (Leah)
Zebulun   -   "
Joseph   -   (Rachel)
Benjamin -   "

The 12 Apostles (Disciples)

Simon (Peter)
Andrew
James (Son of Zebedee)
John   "   "   "
Philip
Bartholomew
Thomas
Matthew (Publican)
James (Son of Alphaeus)
Lebbaeus (Surname Thaddaeus)
Simon (Canaanite)
Judas Iscariot

New Bethel Baptist Church
Sandy Island, S.C.

From the Beginning to Now

A Bible Summary

Male, Female created	Genesis 1:27
Man Formed	" 2:7
" "	I Timothy 2:13
God planted garden in Eden, placed man	Genesis 2:8
Eve formed	" 2:21-23
Fruit of tree in midst of garden	" 3:13
Cain and Abel Born	" 4:1,2
Cain slew Abel	" 4:8
Cain and wife in land of Nod	" 4:16,17
Seth born	" 4:25
Daughters & sons born to Adam & Eve	" 5:3,4
Noah born	" 5:29
Noah begat Shem, Ham, Japheth	" 5:32
Sons of God took daughters of men	" 6:2-4
Repented Lord that he made man	" 6:6,7
All flesh corrupted earth	" 6:12
The Flood	" 7: - 8:
Covenant of rainbow	" 9 :, 9:11
Shed man's blood-man shed your blood	" 9:6
" " " " " " "	Lev. 24:21
	Deut. 19:11-13, Num. 35:16-34
All Nations blessed in Abraham	Genesis 18:18,
	22:18, 26:4
Abram very rich	Genesis 13:2
Jacob very wealthy	" 30:43
Jacob name changed to Israel	" 32:28,
" " " " "	" 35:10
Jacob's 12 sons	" 35:22-26
Manasseh, Ephraim born–Joseph & Asenath	" 41:51,52
Israel's Prophecy; 12 tribes, latter days	" 49:
Sons of Ishmael, etc.	" 25:13,
" " " "	" 37:25-28
Midwives ordered to kill Hebrew sons	Exodus 1:16
Moses slew Egyptian smiting brethren	" 2:11,12

Moses married Zipporah an Ethiopian	Exodus 2:21
" " " " "	Numbers 12:1
Burning bush – Moses out of Egypt	Exodus 3:
Let my people go	" 5:
JEHOVAH, my name	" 6:3
" " "	Psalms 83:18
Passover – Jan. 14-21	Exodus 12:18
430 years in Egypt	" 12:40
10 Commandments	" 20:
" "	Deut. 5:
Sabbath	Exodus 20:10,
"	Exodus 31:15, 34:21, 35:2

Clean – Unclean Animals	Leviticus 11:
" " " Deut. 14:	
Be Holy, I am Holy	" 11:44-45,
" " " " "	I Peter 1:15-16
Unlawful Sexual Relations	Leviticus 18:
Personal Conduct	" 19:
Man lie with mankind as lieth with woman	" 20:13,
" " " " " " " "	" 18:22
Blessings	" 26:1-15
1Tithes of herd, flock	" 27:32-34

Book of wars of the Lord	Numbers 21:14

God is a consuming fire	Deuteronomy 4:24
" " " " "	Hebrews 12:29
Mixed marriages	Deuteronomy 7:3
" "	Ezra 9:12
Into a good land, lack nothing	Deuteronomy 8:7-9
Prophet rise up among brethren	" 18:15-22
Adultery – Rape – Chastity	" 22:5, 21-30
Every man die for own sin	" 24:16,
" " " " " "	Ezekiel 18:17-18
Divorce (Moses)	Deuteronomy 24:

Blessings – Curses	Deuteronomy	28:,11:26-28
Be the head, not the tail	"	28:13
Oppressed and Crushed always	"	28:32-34
Nation against thee	"	28:49
God hide his face – Evil upon us	"	31:17,18 32:20
Evil befall you in latter days	"	31:29
Provoke them to anger with		
foolish nation	"	32:21
		Romans 10:19
Terror within –		
Nation void of counsel	"	32:35 32:28
Joshua succeeds Moses	Joshua	1:
Book of Jasher	"	10:13
Choose this day, God you		
will serve	"	24:15
Judges succeeds Joshua	Judges	1:
Prey, golden earings –		
Ishmaelites	"	8:24
Sampson and Delilah	"	16:
Ruth a good woman	Ruth	1:
People wanted a king	I Samuel	8:19
Saul chosen as king and rejected	"	10: - 12:
Kenites	"	15:6
David anointed as king	"	16:
Book of Jasher	II Samuel	1:18
David appoints Solomon king	I Kings	1: 2:
Solomon had 700 wives		
+ 300 concubines	"	11:3
Elijah to heaven in whirlwind	II Kings	2:11
Manasseh is punished	"	21:

Book of Nathan and Gad	I Chronicles 29:29
Written prophecy visions	
Ahijah, Iddo	II Chronicles 9:29,
	13:22
Book of Shemaiah	" 12:15
Book of Jehu	" 20:34
Mixed marriages	Ezra 9:12
" "	Deuteronomy 7:3
Mixed marriages	Nehemiah 13:23-27
Down to grave, up no more	Job 7:9-10
Man born of woman –	
full of trouble	" 14:1
Days in prosperity,	
years in pleasure	" 36:11
Wicked gone –	
meek inherit earth	Psalm 37:
Evildoers will be destroyed	" 52:-60:
Bloody deceitful men	" 55:23
Wicked estranged from womb	" 58:3
End of wicked	" 73:
Foundations of earth, out of course	" 82:5
Ye are gods – but die like men	" 82:6,7
God is everlasting, eternal,	
Alfa-Omega	" 90:2
	Rev. 1:7-8
To God Glory, Praise, raise up poor	" 113:
Fools despise wisdom and	
instruction	Proverbs 1:7, 22
Envy not the oppressor	" 3:31
Water out of own well, own cistern	" 5:15

Fire in bosom, clothes not burned	Proverbs	6:27
Commit adultery, destroy own soul	"	6:32
Destruction of poor is their poverty	"	10:15
Wealth by vanity diminished – labor	"	13:11
Dog return to vomit – fool to his folly	"	26:11
Door on hinges, slothful upon his bed	"	26:14
Tilleth his land – plenty of bread	"	28:19
		12:11,13:18
Iron sharpeneth iron; correct your son	Proverbs 27:17,
	22:6, 29:17

Nothing new under the sun	Ecclesiastes 1:9,10
No remembrance of former things	"	1:11
To every thing a season, and a time	"	3:
Enjoy good of all your labour	"	3:13
No just man on earth	"	7:20
Living dog better than dead lion	"	9:4, 5
Dust return to earth – spirit to God	"	12:7

I am black	Song of Solomon 1:5,6
" " "	Jeremiah	8:21

Women rule them, cause thee to err	Isaiah	3:12
Wolf dwell with lamb, lion, child	"	11:6-9
Day of Lord – Destruction	"	13:6
Land shadowing wings	"	18:1
Ephraim condemned - drunkards	"	28:
		Hosea
Precept upon precept, line upon line	"	28:10 –13
Sins blotteth out	"	43:25,
" " "	"	44:22
There is no other Lord	"	44: - 45:
I make peace, and create evil	"	45:7
		Amos 3:6
No peace, saith my God, to the wicked	"	48:22,57:21
Blind, dumb, ignorant, greedy dogs	"	56:10-11

People destroyed for lack of knowledge	Hosea 4:
Ephraim – Iniquity	" 4:-13:
	Isaiah 28:
Israel's pride – Punishment	Hosea 7:-10:
Ephraim's glory gone	" 9:11
Return, Israel	" 14:
Day of Lord – Darkness – Punishment	Joel
" " " " "	Amos 5:18-20
Punishment of Nations, Israel	Amos 1:-9:
Evil in the city, the Lord done it	" 3:6
God revealeth in secret to servant, prophets	" 3:7
Nation raised up against house of Israel	" 6:14
" " " " " " "	Jere. 5:15
Famine – latter day	Amos 8:11
God restores his people	" 9:
House, top of mountain	Micah 4:
End time vision –	" 4:
Chaldeans strong nation	Habakkuk 1:-2:
Afflicted and poor people	Zephaniah 3:12
Woe to Nations – Prophets, Priests	" 1:-3:
Earneth wages put into bag with holes	Haggai 1:6
Visions of Zechariah	Zechariah 3:-6:
Plague to people who fought Jerusalem	" 14:12
God loved Jacob, hated Esau	Malachi 1:2,3
" " " " "	Romans 9:13
Priests cursed and dung in face	Malachi 2:1-10
God doesn't change	" 3:6
Will a man rob God	" 3:8
Tithes into storehouse	" 3:10

The Beatitudes, light shine, salt of earth	Matthew 5:
Be perfect	" 5:48
" "	Hebrews 6:
Lay not up treasures on earth	Matthew 6:19
Ask, Seek, Knock	" 7:7
Our Father's prayer	" 9:13
12 Apostles	" 10:2-
Come unto me, take my yoke	" 11:28-30
Your brethren - Your Father	" 12:48-50,
	23:9
Parable of seed (field, tares)	" 13:37-40
" " " " "	Luke 8:5-
Remarriage forbidden, ex spouse alive	" 19:3-9,
" " " " "	Romans 7:2-3
Signs of end – false prophets	Matthew 24:
" " " " "	Mk.13: Lu.21:
Parable of 10 virgins – Be Profitable	Matthew 25:1-
	13, 30
Separation of sheep and goats	" 25:31-46
Nothing hid - Secrets revealed	Mark 4:22
Devils cast into swine	" 5:13
In vain they worship me-man's tradition	" 7:7
Authority of government	" 12:
Signs of end - false prophets	" 13:
Foretold all things	" 13:23
Gabriel visits Mary	Luke 1:
No prophet accepted in his country	" 4:24
" " " " " "	John 4:44
Judging others – every tree known by fruit	" 6:
Mission of the seventy	" 10:
Who is your neighbor	" 10:29-37
Gulf – Fixed	" 16:26
Rich man and Lazarus	" 16:

Signs of end - false prophets	Luke	21:
Jerusalem compassed with armies	"	21:20
Cloud – Coming in a cloud	"	21:27,
" " " " "	"	24:51
Man must be born again	John	3:3-5,
" " " " "		I Peter 1:23
Everlasting life	John	3:16
God is a Spirit	"	4:24
Dead shall hear	"	5:25-29
The Light of the world	"	8:12
The truth shall make you free	"	8:32
Ye are of your father the devil	"	8:44
Many mansions	"	14:2
I am the way, the truth, and life	"	14:6
If you love me, keep my commandments	"	14:15
Comforter	"	14:26,
"	"	15:26
The True Vine	"	15:
One lost, son of perdition	"	17:12
Cloud – Coming in a cloud	Acts	1:11,
" " " " "		I Th. 4:17
Last days, my Spirit upon all flesh	"	2:17
The Day of Pentecost	"	2:
In bondage 400 years – Book of Prophets	"	7:6,7, 42
Simon bewitched people with sorceries	"	8:9-11
God dwelleth not in temples – hands	"	7:48,17:24,
" " " " " "		I Cor. 3:16
One blood all nations of men	"	17:26
Resurrection of dead - just & unjust	"	24:15
" " " " " "		I Cor. 15:35-
Gay lifestyles	Romans	1:26,27
" "		I Cor. 6:9
God shows no partiality	"	2:11

93

Remarriage forbidden, ex spouse alive	Romans	7:2-3
" " " " "		Matt. 19:3-9
Sons of God have spirit of God	Romans	8:14
Faith by hearing	"	10:17
" " "		Heb. 1:11
Spirit of slumber – blindness	"	11:7,8,25
Owe no man	"	13:8
Unrighteous not inherit kingdom	I Corinthians	6:9-10
Problems of marriage, divorce	"	7:
Remarriage forbidden, ex spouse alive	"	7:10,11,39
" " " " "		Romans 7:2-3
Spiritual gifts	"	12:
God not author of confusion	"	14:33
Women keep silence in churches	"	14:34-35
" " " " "		I Tim. 2:11-13
Resurrection of dead	"	15:35-58
We are all changed at last trump	"	15:51-52
Absent from body, present with God,	II Corinthians	5:8
Soweth – Reap sparingly, bountifully	"	9:6
Satan as angel of light, his ministers	"	11:14
Third heaven	"	12:2
Sons of God, not slaves	Galatians	4:6,7
Abraham sons, bondwoman		
and freewoman	"	4:22
Works of flesh	"	5:19-21
Whatsoever a man soweth, shall he reap	"	6:7
Grace through faith saves	Ephesians	2:8,9
Renewed spirit of mind, new man	"	4:23-28
Be Righteous with True Holiness	"	4:24,
" " " " "		Lev. 11:44-45
Wives submit	Ephesians	5:22-33
" "		Colossians 3:18

Spiritual wickedness in high places   Ephesians   6:12

To live is Christ, to die gain   Philippians 1:21-23
Work out your own salvation   "   2:12
Sons of God, midst of crooked nation   "   2:15

Traditions of men   Colossians   2:8
New man – renewed in knowledge   "   3:10
   "   "   "   "   "   Ephesians 4:23

Jews killed Jesus   I Thessalonians 2:15
Caught in clouds   "   4:17
Resurrection   "   4:13-18
Abstain from all appearance of evil   "   5:22

Lord Jesus revealed from Heaven II Thessalonians 1:7
Resurrection   "   1:7
   "   "   2:1-8
Let no man deceive you   "   2:3
God send them strong delusion   "   2:11
No work no eat
 (Work & Eat your own Bread)   "   3:10-12

Contrary to sound doctrine   I Timothy   1:10
One mediator   "   2:5
Suffer not a woman to teach   "   2:11-13
   "   "   "   "   "   "   I Cor 14:34-35
Every creature of God is good, men   I Timothy 4:3,4
   "   "   "   "   "   "   "   Acts 10:12-19,28
Provide for own, not infidel   I Timothy   5:8
Love of money is root of all evil   "   6:10

Spirit of power, love, sound mind   II Timothy   1:7
Study and rightly divide word   "   2:15
Last days perilous times shall come   "   3:
Ever learning – never, knowledge of truth   "   3:7

95

All scripture by inspiration of God	II Timothy	3:16
Eternal life God promised	Titus	1:2
Duties of elders, deacons, bishops	"	1:
Aged women teach young women	"	2:
Milk v. meat	Hebrews	5:13,14
Order of Melchisedec	"	5:-6:
Move on to perfection, after saved	"	6:
Appointed unto men once to die	"	9:27
Faith	"	11:1
"	Romans	10:17
Cloud of witnesses	Hebrews	12:1
God is a consuming fire	"	12:29
Double minded man is unstable	James	1:8
God tempteth no man	"	1:13
Every good and perfect gift is from above	"	1:17
Pure religion	"	1:27
Faith, no works, is dead	"	2:17-26
Wisdom from above is pure, peaceable	"	3:17
Submit to God, resist devil, he will flee	"	4:7
Born through God's word	I Peter	1:17-25
Be holy, I am holy	"	1:15-16
Christ preached to spirits in prison	"	3:19
Days of Noah, 8 souls saved	"	3:20
Younger submit to the elder	"	5:5,6
Prophecy came by holy men of God	II Peter	1:21
False prophets	"	2:-22
" "	Ezekiel	13:, 34:
Old world spared not	II Peter	2:4,5
World that was – perished	"	3:6
One day with Lord – thousand years	"	3:8

Elements melt, new heaven, new earth   II Peter 3:10-13

Cain, was of that wicked one	I John	3:12
Love not in word, tongue, deed & truth	"	3:18
God is love (true love)	"	4:8
The Father, the Word, the Holy Ghost	"	5:7

Don't be partaker of evil deeds   II John   1:11

Out of Egypt and destroyed	Jude	1:5
Angels left habitation and destroyed	"	1:6

He cometh with clouds, Alfa-Omega	Revelation	1:7,8
Letters to seven churches	"	1:-3:
Receive according to your works	"	2:23,
" " " " "	"	20:12,13
" " " " "	"	22:12
Church of Philadelphia, open door	"	3:7
Hour of temptation, upon all the world	"	3:10
I stand at door and knock – open the door	"	3:20
Four and twenty elders at throne	"	4:
Seven Seals	"	5:-8:
One fourth of men killed	"	6:8
All nations, people, kindreds, tongues	"	7:1-9
Out of great tribulation	"	7:14
Seventh Seal, Seven Angels	"	8:-11:
Seal of God in forehead	"	9:4
Third part of men slain	"	9:15
Two witnesses – forty and two months	"	11:
7th angel sounded – 7th trump	"	11:15
War in Heaven – 7 heads, 10 horns, dragon	"	12:
Beast from sea – forty and two months, 666	"	13:
144,000 – Babylon is fallen	"	14:
Seven Vials, 7 last plagues – Armageddon	"	15:-16:
Babylon, mother of harlots, abominations	"	17:
7 heads (mountains), 10 horns (kings)	"	17:

The Doom of Babylon	Revelation	18:
" " " "	"	14:8
Babylon's sorceries deceived all nations	"	18:23
Alleluia; Salvation and glory	"	19:
Satan bound -First Resurrection-	"	20:
Millennium	"	20:
Great white throne – second death	"	20:
New Heaven, New Earth	"	21:1
Some in lake of fire – second death	"	21:8
Holy Jerusalem, 12 gates, 12 tribes	"	21:
Twelve manner of fruits	"	22:2
Reward every man according to his work	"	22:12,
" " " " " " " "		20:12
" " " " " ' "		Psalm 62:12

Blessed, keep prophecy,
Do Commandments   Revelation   22:7,14

8 Days in The Beginning

The Seven Seals

A Bible Timeline

THE BEGINNING

In the beginning God created the heaven and the earth. (Genesis 1:1)

DAY 1 - Night (darkness) and Day (light) created.

DAY 2 - God made firmament, and called firmament heaven.

DAY 3 - Dry land appear (Earth) and waters under heaven gathered together (Seas). Earth brought forth grass, herb yielding seed, tree yielding fruit.

DAY 4 - God made two great lights, greater light to rule the day, and the lesser light to rule the night. Lights for signs, seasons, for days and years.

DAY 5 - God created great whales, and every living creature that moveth, and every winged fowl.

DAY 6 - God made beast and cattle and every thing that creepeth upon earth. God created man in his own image, in the image of God created he him; male and female created he them. (Genesis 1:27)

DAY 7 - God rested on the seventh day and blessed the seventh day. (Genesis 2:1-3)

DAY 8 - God formed man of the dust of the ground. (Genesis 2:7) God planted a garden in Eden; and put the man.   (Genesis 2:8) God made a woman (Eve) from man (Adam). (Genesis 2:20-25)

God said, don't eat of the tree which is in the midst of the garden. (Genesis 3:3)

Eve said, the serpent beguiled me, and I did eat. (Genesis 3:13)

Cain and Abel born. (Genesis 4:1)
Cain slew Abel. (Genesis 4:8)
Cain went and dwelt in the land of Nod. (Genesis 4:16)

Seth born to Adam and Eve. (Genesis 4:25) After Seth born Adam lived 800 years and begat sons and daughters. (Genesis 5:4) Adam lived 930 years. (Genesis 5:5)

Methuselah born. (Genesis 5:21)   Methuselah lived 969 years. (Genesis 5:27)

Noah born. (Genesis 5:28,29)
Noah was 500 years old and begat Shem, Ham, and Japheth. (Genesis 5:32)

The sons of God took wives of the daughters of men, and they bare children to them. (Genesis 6:2-4)

God told Noah to make an ark of gopher wood. (Genesis 6:14)
Flood waters dries up in year 601 on first day of first month. (Genesis 8:13)

Abram born. (Genesis 11:26)   In thee all families of the earth be blessed. (Genesis 12:3)   Abram 86 years old when Hagar (Egyptian) bare Ishmael to Abram. (Genesis 16:16)
God changes Abram name to Abraham. (Genesis 17:5)
Ishmael shall begat 12 princes and be a great nation. (Genesis 17:20)

Abraham was 100 years old when Isaac born. (Genesis 21:5)

Isaac was 40 years old when he took Rebekah to wife. Two nations in womb of Rebekah. Esau and Jacob. (Genesis 25:20-27)

Jacob and Rachel begat Joseph. (Genesis 30:22-24) God changes Jacob's name to Israel. (Genesis 32:28) Jacob had 12 sons. (Genesis 35:22-26)   Joseph sold into Egypt. (Genesis 37:36)

Manasseh and Ephraim born to Joseph and Asenath in Egypt. (Genesis 41:51,52)
Jacob (Israel) and 66 souls go into Egypt to Joseph. (Genesis 46:26)

Moses leads children of Israel (Jacob) out of Egypt. (Exodus) Moses had Ethiopian wife named Zipporah (Numbers 12:1)

David becomes king over Israel.
David makes his son Solomon king over Israel.
 (I Chronicles 23:1)

Christ is born.
Signs of the End. (Matthew 24: Mark 13: Luke 21:)

Antichrist comes. (6th seal, 6th trump) (Daniel 7:25, 8:25, 11:21) (Rev. 5:-13:) 666

The Seven Vials – Seven last plagues - (Revelation 16:)

Armageddon – (Revelation 16:16)

Christ returns - (7th seal, 7th trump) We shall all be changed. (I Corinthians 15:51)

First resurrection – **millennium.**   (Revelation 20:3-7)

Great white throne judgment.   (Revelation 20:11-15)

Second death.   (Revelation 20:14, 21:8)

NEW HEAVEN, NEW EARTH.   (Revelation 21:1)

Holy Jerusalem descending out of heaven from God. (Revelation 21:10)

Tree of life, twelve manner of fruits.   (Revelation 22:2)

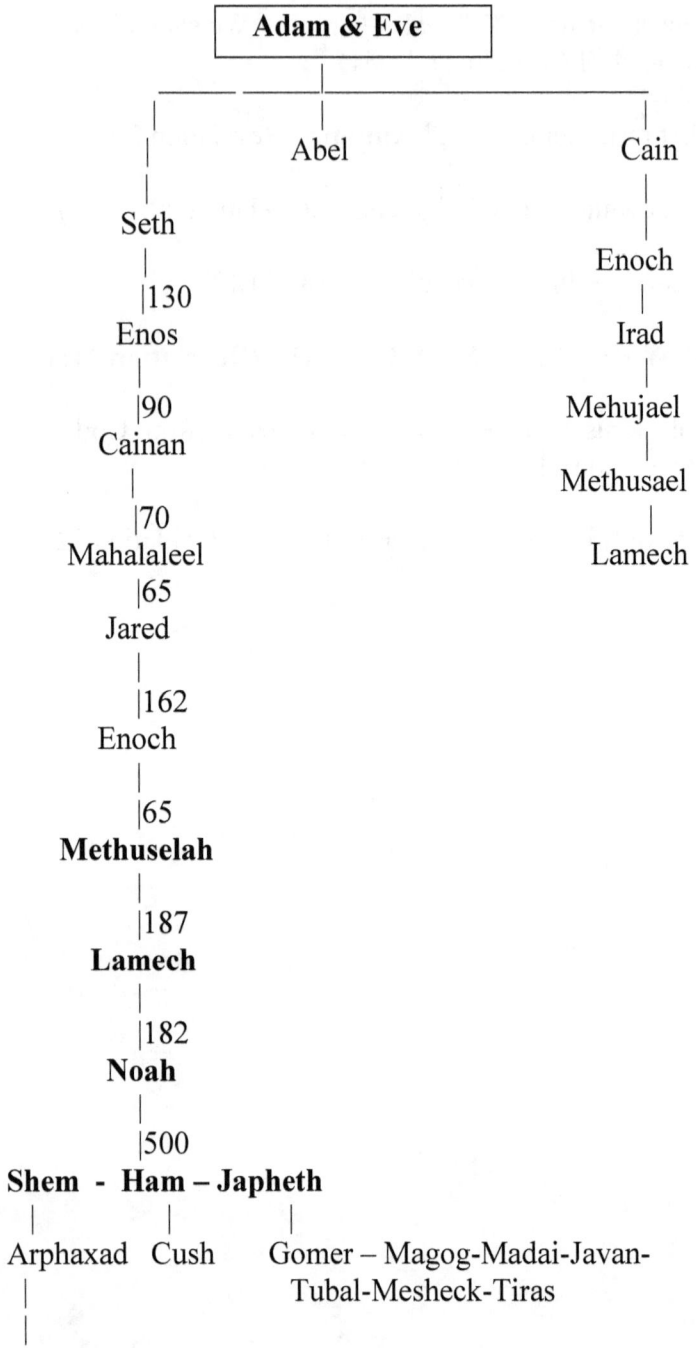

```
                    ┌──────────────────┐
                    │   Adam & Eve     │
                    └──────────────────┘
         ┌───────────────────┼──────────────────────┐
         │               Abel                       │
         │                                         Cain
        Seth                                         │
         │                                        Enoch
        |130                                         │
        Enos                                        Irad
         │                                           │
        |90                                       Mehujael
       Cainan                                        │
         │                                      Methusael
        |70                                          │
     Mahalaleel                                   Lamech
        |65
       Jared
         │
        |162
       Enoch
         │
        |65
    Methuselah
         │
        |187
      Lamech
         │
        |182
       Noah
         │
        |500
   Shem  -  Ham – Japheth
     │       │        │
  Arphaxad  Cush    Gomer – Magog-Madai-Javan-
     │               Tubal-Mesheck-Tiras
     │
```

104

|
Terah
|
Abraham   (Abraham later married Kenturah,
| Genesis 25:1)
|
Isaac   (Ishmael is son by Hagar the Egyptian,
| Genesis 6:16, 21:9)
|
Esau – Jacob   (Esau is Edom, Genesis 36:)
            |
            |
        Ruben, Simeon, Levi, Judah, Zebulun, Issachar
          (sons by Leah)
        Dan, Naphtali (sons by Bilhah)
        Gad, Asher (sons by Zilpah)
        Joseph, Benjamin (sons by Rachel)
                    Manasseh & Ephraim (sons of
                    Joseph & Asenath in Egypt)
                      Levi begat Kohath & Kohath begat
                      Amram & Amram begat <u>Moses</u>
        Judas (son of Jacob)   (Moses married
                      Zipporah an Ethiopian, Numbers 12:1)

    Phares

    Esrom

    Aram

    Animadab

    Naasson

    Salmon

    Boaz

Boaz   (Boaz married Ruth a Moabitess, Ruth 4:13)

Obed

Jesse

David   (14 Generations from Abraham to David)
         (David's Children, II Samuel 3:-5)

Solomon   (Bathsheba is mother of Solomon,
           I Kings 1:10, 2:22)

Roboam

Abia

Asa

Josaphat

Joram

Ozias

Joatham

Achaz

Ezekias

Manasses

Amon

Josias

Jechonias   (carried away to Babylon – 14 Generations
                  from David)

Salathiel

Zorobabel

 Abiud

Eliakim

 Azor

 Sadoc

 Achim

 Eliud

Eleazar

Matthan

 Jacob

Joseph - Mary

Christ   (14 Generations from carrying away into
                   Babylon)

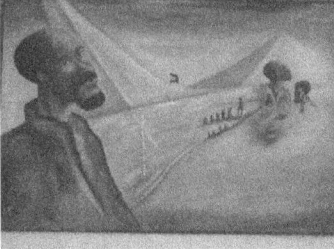

Be Renewed in the spirit of your mind
Put on the New Man
Get Renewed in Knowledge
Ephesians 4:23-24, Colossians 3:10

Bible Questions

And ye shall know the truth, and the truth shall make you free. (John 8:32)

Jesus was not born in the month of December. (Luke 1:)

The Sabbath day is the seventh (7th) day. (Exodus 3:15, 20:10, 34:21, 35:2)

The genesis of Adam and Eve goes back 6,000 years. (Genesis 2:7)
   (back to the 8th day, not back to the 6th day)
   God planted a garden in Eden on the 8th day and placed man there. (Genesis 2:8)

Who were the male and female created on the 6th day? (Genesis 1:27)

After Cain slew Abel, Cain took a wife in the land of Nod. (Genesis 4:16,17)
   Adam and Eve didn't have a daughter until after Seth was born.
   Who were the people in the land of Nod?

The sons of God took the daughters of men for wives and they had children. (Genesis 6:2-4)
   Who were these sons of God?

Who were the beings on earth before Adam and Eve?

Do Angels have wings? (Genesis 1:26)

What fruit did Eve pick from the tree in the midst of the garden? (Genesis 3:6)

Who is the tree in the midst of the garden? (Genesis 3:3)

Will Christians fly away to heaven? (Ezekiel 13:18, Revelation 21:1-)

What is the genesis of the people who placed the children of Israel in bondage?

Is the devil the father of Cain? (John 8:44)
   Were Cain and Abel twins? (Genesis 4:1,2)

What are the letters saying to the seven churches? (Revelation 1:-3:)

Who takes part in the first resurrection? (Revelation 20:4,5)

What happens in the millennium? (Revelation 20:)
Will we recognize our relatives in the millennium? (Ezekiel 44:25)

When does the great white throne judgment occur? (Revelation 20:11)

Who takes part in the second death? (Revelation 20:13-15, 21:8)

When does the new heaven and new earth appear? (Revelation 21:1)

How are we rewarded? (Revelation 20:12, 22:12)

Are we living in the fig tree generation? What half? What quarter?

110

Where will your prophet come from? What will he look like? (Deuteronomy 18:15-22)

And ye shall know the truth, and the truth shall make you free. (John 8:32)

He that tilleth his land shall have plenty of bread: but he that followeth after vain persons shall have poverty enough. (Proverbs 28:19)

As a dog returneth to his vomit, so a fool returneth to his folly. (Proverbs 26:11)

As the door turneth upon his hinges, so doth the slothful upon his bed. (Proverbs 26:14)

Ye are of your father the devil, and the lusts of your father ye will do. He was a murderer from the beginning, and abode not in the truth, because there is no truth in him. When he speaketh a lie, he speaketh of his own: for he is a liar, and the father of it. (John 8:44)

I will also leave in the midst of thee an afflicted and poor people, and they shall trust in the name of the Lord. (Zephaniah 3:12)

As for Ephraim, their glory shall fly away like a bird, from the birth, and from the womb, and from the conception. (Hosea 9:11)

Likewise, ye younger, submit yourselves unto the elder. Yea, all of you be subject one to another, and be clothed with humility: for God resisted the proud, and giveth grace to the humble. (I Peter 5:5)

Be not deceived; God is not mocked: for whatsoever a man soweth, that shall he also reap. (Galatians 6:7)

For there is not a just man upon earth, that doeth good, and sinneth not. (Ecclesiastes 7:20)

Submit yourselves therefore to God. Resist the devil, and he will flee from you. (James 4:7)

Behold, I shew you a mystery; we shall not all sleep, but we shall all be changed. (I Corinthians 15:51)

Remain Anchored on a Solid Foundation

Subsequent generations must remain anchored on the same **Solid Foundation** that the Bible Belt generation and the Civil Rights Movement was anchored on; anchored on a **Deep and Abiding Faith and Belief in God!** People marched and died in the streets so that we could have better opportunities and attend schools of our choice. Subsequent generations have a **Moral Obligation and Duty** to march down the hallways of the schools, and to sit in the classrooms, Study and Work to **Obtain Economic Skills,** and move on up the Economic Ladder to the Mountain Top. The Mountain Top is still there a-top the Economic Ladder, so you'll need Economic Skills to climb the Economic Ladder to get to the Mountain Top.

The Children of Disobedience

Many of the youngsters at this day at this point in time are acting as if the world is revolving around them. They have their own value system complete with their loud music and fancy clothes and their own agenda. The children of disobedience are attempting to leap over their prior generation on the learning curve; not realizing that they are setting up their own destruction and downfall. By not seeking and heeding the advice and consultation of responsible adults, they are in effect limiting and reducing their options. They are making critical decisions without consulting with responsible adults, and then trying to get responsible adults to ratify and support their unwise decisions. There are obstacles on the learning curve of life; and responsible adults can help the young generation as they travel on the learning curve.

We are in a spiritual war; "Wherein in time past ye walked according to the course of this world, according to the prince of the power of the air, the spirit that now worketh in the children of disobedience" (Ephesians 2:2). We must all "put on the whole armour of God, that ye may be able to stand against the wiles of the devil". "For we wrestle not against flesh and blood, but against principalities, against powers, against the rulers of the darkness of this world, against spiritual wickedness in high places" (Ephesians 6:11-13). Some are defiled and unbelieving, even their mind and conscience is defiled (Titus 1:15). "For which thing's sake the wrath of God cometh on the children of disobedience" (Colossians 3:6). Even though you may have been alienated, you can be reconciled (Colossians 1:21).

"And you hath he quickened, who were dead in trespasses and sins" (Ephesians 2:1). "And have put on the new man, which is renewed in knowledge after the image of him that created him" (Colossians 3:10). **Be renewed in the spirit of your mind,** you were created in righteousness and true holiness (Ephesians 4:23-24).

There are blessings for obedience to the word of God, and curses for disobedience to the word of God (Deuteronomy 28:1-68). We can all be blessed (Revelation 22:14). Stop, and Listen, and be **Doers** of the word, and get to the conclusion of the whole matter (James 1:22-25, Ecclesiastes 12:13).

Remain Focused on Goals and Objectives and Practice
Financial Accountability

T-Accounts will Become Unbalanced when Cluttered With Off-the-Wall Nonsense and Detrimental Distractions

Benefits	Detrimental Distractions
Romans 11:8 – Owe no man	Loud Music
Proverbs 10:15 – The destruction of the poor is their poverty	Cell Phones ?
	$100 Dollar Tennis Shoes
Proverbs 22:7 – The borrower is servant to the lender	Low Baggy Pants
	Tight Pants
Romans 12:11 – Not slothful in business	Drugs & Alcohol
II Corinthians 6:14-18 – Be ye not unequally yoked together with unbelievers	Empty Heads
	Hip Hop Culture ?
Ephesians 4:23-24 – Be renewed in the spirit of your mind	Cyber Space dot ... com
Colossians 3:10 – Put on the new man, renewed in knowledge	Ignorance
Come to	J E S U S

Study and Stay in School and Acquire
Economic Skills
And Move on Up

Knowledge is Power – Study and Work

PRACTICE TRUTH – TEACH TRUTH – KNOW THE TRUTH

For it is written that each of you will be rewarded according to your works.
And faith without works is dead; therefore, your works must manifest your faith. Practice Truth – Teach Truth – Know the Truth.
If you don't Practice Truth, you cannot sit with me in my booth.
Many people seeking relief from stresses of the day get caught in snares.
And are popping pills and drinking alcohol all up and down the boulevard.
Clouds of people caught in snares roaming around with their absent guard.
Playing around and finger popping at juke joints up and down the boulevard.
Young people in pain hooked on mind twisters, living a life so very hard.
Popping pills in the Devil's Den, they've dealt themselves a terrible card.
Beware; it is a surety, that according to your works you shall be rewarded.

Work is essential, for you can only reap what you have sown.
Seeds on good ground will triumph and you'll see what you have grown.
So till your land, and you will surely have a good harvest in your yard.
And won't feel the pain of those on mind twisters down on the boulevard.
And accelerate going back down to a quick return to the dust of the ground.

Partying won't do, for according to your works you shall
be rewarded.
Our works must be based on truth to avoid the pitfalls
on the boulevard.
So Practice Truth – Teach Truth – Know the Truth! You
are seed on good ground.

There's a terrible storm full of pain all up and down the
boulevard.
People caught up on mind twisters, tears raining,
pushing them down.
The Devil's in his Den with his snares, keeping them
down on the ground.
If they don't rise up soon, they'll quickly return to the
dust of the ground.
So stand up where you are, make it better, and you'll
receive a good card.
And see clearly as the light brightens the way, for within
you is your guard.
And your guard within will brighten the way and you'll
see very clearly, and avoid the snares in the Devil's Den
all up and down the boulevard.

I judge not any man, but it is written that if any would
not work, neither should he eat. Therefore, if you don't
practice truth you cannot sit with me in my booth. For
you will be rewarded according to your works and reap
what you have sown. Practice Truth – Teach Truth –
Know The Truth!
For you shall reap what you have sown.

And unto the man he said, Behold, the fear of the Lord, that is wisdom; and to depart from evil is understanding. Job 28:28.

The fear of the Lord is the beginning of wisdom: a good understanding have all they that do his commandments: his praise endureth for ever. Psalm 111:10.

Ask, and it shall be given you; seek, and ye shall find; knock, and it shall be opened unto you: St. Matthew 7:7.

Because strait is the gate, and narrow is the way, which leadeth unto life, and few there be that find it. St. Matthew 7:14.

Not every one that saith unto me, Lord, Lord, shall enter into the kingdom of heaven; but he that doeth the will of my Father which is in heaven. St. Matthew 7:21.

THERE'S ONLY ONE WAY TO THE TREE OF LIFE;
LISTEN, AND HEAR THE CONCLUSION OF THE WHOLE
MATTER! St. John 14:6, Ecclesiastes 12:13, Revelation 22:14

Observe & DO All The
Commandments & Statutes
Deuteronomy 28:1-2, Ecclesiastes 12:13
Revelation 22:14

Faith-Works
James 2:17-26
Revelation 20:12, 22:12

Milk v. Meat
Hebrews 5:13-14
Isaiah 28:9-10
I Corinthians 3:2

Holy-Righteous
Leviticus 11:44-45
I Peter 1:15-16

Wisdom, Knowledge
& Understanding
Proverbs 4:7, 2:6, 3:5

Saved
St. John 3:16-17

Born Again
St. John 3:3
I Peter 1:23

T.J. Pyatt
04

Revelation 22:2

122

There's Only One Way to the Tree of Life; Listen, and Hear The Conclusion of the Whole Matter!
St. John 14:6, Ecclesiastes 12:13, Revelation 22:14

Observe and Do All The
Commandments and Statutes
Deuteronomy 28:1-2, Ecclesiastes 12:13
Revelation 22:14

Faith-Works
James 2:17-26
Revelation 20:12, 22:12

Milk v. Meat
Hebrews 5:13-14
Isaiah 28:9-10
I Corinthians 3:2

Holy-Righteous
Leviticus 11:44-45
I Peter 1:15-16

Wisdom, Knowledge
& Understanding
Proverbs 4:7, 2:6, 3:5

Saved
St. John 3:16-17

Born Again
St. John 3:3
I Peter 1:23

Blessed are they that do his commandments,
that they may have right to the tree of life, and
may enter in through the gates into the city.
Revelation 22:14.

I am the door: by me if any man enter in, he shall be saved, and shall go in and out, and find pasture. St. John 10:9

Jesus saith unto him, I am the way, the truth, and the life: no man cometh unto the Father, but by me. St. John 14:6

Come to Jesus! – Jesus Can Help You!

As we get deeper into these latter days with so much chaos, problems and confusion all over the world, many people are feeling overwhelmed and stressed out. They even see and feel more difficult days ahead with no relief in sight; and there are indeed some dark and cloudy days ahead as we journey on deeper into these latter days. Many people are seeking peace and tranquility, relief from the stresses and strains of world events that have a negative impact on their daily lives. They have tried seeking relief from institutions, drugs, family reunions, from their family, friends and strangers. Some have formed all types of groups and alliances seeking such relief. But many of them are still stressed out, and heavy laden, with weary souls, and cannot find the rest, peace and tranquility they so desperately seek and need. They are constantly seeking relief.

We were told millenniums ago; **"But, seek ye first the kingdom of God, and his righteousness; and all these things shall be added unto you"** (St. Matthew 6:33). There is Only One Way that we can get what we need to be perfectly content as we get deeper into these latter days. There is Only One Person who can give us what we need. We need only come, **Come to Jesus! Jesus can help you!** There is only one door that leads to peace and tranquility, relief from the stresses and strains, and to a good pasture. Jesus said, **"I am the door: by me if any man enter in, he shall be saved, and shall go in and out, and find pasture"** (St. John 10:9). **"I am the way, the truth, and the life: no man cometh unto the Father, but by me"** (St. John 14:6). There is one God, and one mediator between God and men, the man Christ

Jesus (I Timothy 2:5). Jesus is the true vine, and if we abide in him and his words abide in us, we will bear much fruit (St. John 15:1-7). We can all be blessed (Revelation 22:14).

In the Kingdom of God is everything we need to carry us through these difficult times. The Kingdom of God and poverty are mutually exclusive. There is no confusion in the Kingdom of God. **Blessings are in the Kingdom of God.** You can be the Head, and not the tail, above only and not beneath; but you must fulfill the condition precedent in Deuteronomy 28:13. There is Only One Way to the Kingdom of God, and One Door that you must enter in. Let us not be as the children of disobedience (Ephesians 2:2, 5:6). We need only Ask, Seek and Knock (St. Matthew 7:7).

We must be Doers of the word (James 1:22-25). We must put on the whole armour of God, for we are in a spiritual war (Ephesians 6:11-13). We must put on the shield of faith, take with us the helmet of salvation, and the sword of the Spirit, which is the word of God (Ephesians 6:16-17). You can get a renewed spirit of the mind, and put on the new man (Ephesians 4:23-24, Colossians 3:10). There is only One Way, Truth and Life; one mediator between God and men; one Door, to the Kingdom of God. You can come into the Kingdom of God, just listen to that knock at the door (Revelation 3:20). Just **Come to Jesus! Jesus Can Help You!**

Come unto me, all ye that labour and are heavy laden, and I will give you rest. St. Matthew 11:28

Take my yoke upon you, and learn of me; for I am meek and lowly in heart: and ye shall find rest unto your souls. St. Matthew 11:29

For my yoke is easy, and my burden is light.
St. Matthew 11:30

Come now, and let us reason together, saith the Lord: though your sins be as scarlet, they shall be as white as snow; though they be red like crimson, they shall be as wool. Isaiah 1:18

Behold, I stand at the door, and knock: if any man hear my voice, and open the door, I will come in to him, and will sup with him, and he with me. Revelation 3:20

Behold, I shew you a mystery; We shall not all
sleep, but we shall all be changed,
(I Corinthians 15:51)

In a moment, in the twinkling of an eye, at the
last trump: for the trumpet shall sound, and the
dead shall be raised incorruptible, and we shall
be changed. (I Corinthians 15:52)

Because thou hast kept the word of my patience,
I also will keep thee from the hour of
temptation, which shall come upon all the
world, to try them that dwell upon the earth.
(Revelation 3:10)

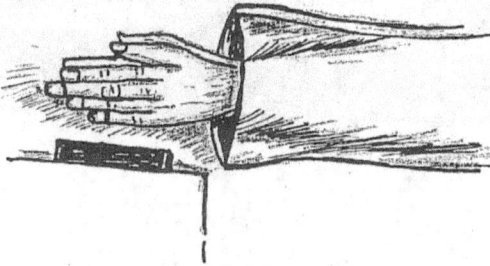

**But take ye heed: behold, I have foretold you
all things.** (St. Mark 13:23)

That View

That is the view as seen from my perspective and vantage point, for over half a century now. We have come a long way on our sojourn here in the Land of Plenty. We must continue on to the mountain top to the promised land; but there is only one who can lead us to that land. It is many of us who have chosen to remain wandering in the wilderness of materialism.

We need only to renew our main focus and remain anchored on solid ground just as our ancestors did. They were anchored on solid ground in that they were anchored in a deep and abiding faith and belief in God.

We must remain anchored on such solid ground, Study and Work, and move on up to the mountaintop. But, **There is Only One Way. AMEN!** St. John 14:6.

Art Director – T.J. Pyatt
www.tjpyatt.com

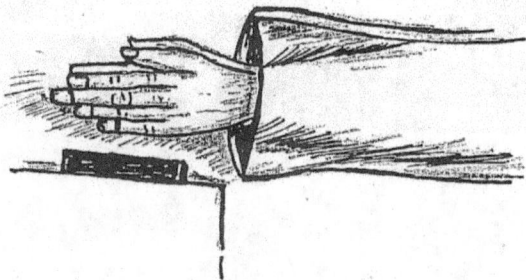

Behold! Behold

There is Only One Way

One Way

Index

There is Only One Way

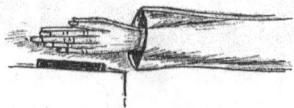

AMEN!

www.ingramcontent.com/pod-product-compliance
Lightning Source LLC
LaVergne TN
LVHW021459080426
835509LV00018B/2347